MAXIMALISM

6	**TASSELS AND TEARS** BY SIMON DOONAN
12	**EXCESS AND EXUBERANCE**
14	**MAXIMALISM**
280	**TIMELINE**
285	**INDEX**

TASSELS AND TEARS
BY SIMON DOONAN

Once upon a time, towards the end of the last century, I crossed the threshold of Dawnridge, the Beverly Hills home of Tony Duquette. A towering eccentric, physically and otherwise, Tony greeted me wearing flowing ecclesiastical robes and an embroidered skull cap. His gnarled hands were encrusted with massive sculptural rings, which looked as if they expected to be kissed.

I was happy to oblige. Tony's storied career entitled him to unlimited adulation. Hollywood set designer, a protégé of Elsie de Wolfe, sculptor, and artist, Duquette created trippy high-voltage sets and interiors, combining opium-den glamour with his own unique brand of upcycling. In alchemist Tony's hands, porcelain electrical conductors became important al fresco sculptures. Crap from studio backlots or the Los Angeles wrecking yards was transformed into delectable *objets trouvés*. Tony was the kind of guy who could take two rusty car mufflers, gold-leaf them, and then suggest you might consider dangling them from your earlobes at your next brunch.

Located on a shady street, the simple, charming entrance to Dawnridge gave no indication of the unhinged visual extravaganza that lay within. Once inside I felt as if my acid had just kicked in. Everywhere I looked, my gaze was consumed by ramparts of antiques, chinoiserie, sunburst sculptures, gold-leafing, tapestries, and things that I have no idea what they were. The richesse and madness were overwhelming. But what made Dawnridge so memorable was, as noted above, the improvisational use of found objects, including a massively grandiose chandelier constructed from plastic drinking glasses and popsicle sticks. This rule-breaking eccentricity, a who-cares-what-the-neighbors-think mentality, is a common trait of the greatest maximalists.

Maximalists have no desire to seek approval from others. Their goal is to hypnotize onlookers into a state of adoring submission. (Kiss those rings!) Maximalist décor puts the viewer on notice: you are here to admire and obey. Think, for example, of Versailles, the primordial muck from which today's maximal interiors have emerged. Louis XIV created his palace with a castration strategy in mind. His goal was to neutralize the threat from the power-hungry regional aristocrats of France. Trapped in Louis' dazzling whirligig, potential rivals were too busy shagging, powdering their wigs, and eating bonbons to stage a coup against the self-styled 'Sun King.' Yes, like many maximalists in this tome, Louis cast himself as a demi-god.

Tony Duquette was more of a wizard than a deity. Once you fell under his spell, the quotidian realities of Los Angeles were magically erased. As I took in Tony's gasp-inducing pad—a true maxi-pad, as it were—I saw no signs of the contemporary world. No stray cans of Pledge. No dreary extension cords or electrical outlets. No half-eaten Twix or stray packs of ciggies. No signs of coupon clipping. The realities of day-to-day existence? Gone. This is one of the niftiest aspects of maximalism: the ability to torpedo reality. Faced with the white-hot glare of the maximalist blow torch, the dreary mundanities of life run screaming in the opposite direction. Hookers in boob tubes and Guess jeans plied their trade on Sunset. On Fairfax, chunky waitresses sloshed coffee into hearty mugs at Canters Deli. Meanwhile over at Dawnridge, Tony Duquette—Edith Sitwell meets Liberace meets Alexander Liberman—wafts from room to room like an ancient mystic.

After a riveting chat with charmer Tony and his wife Beegle, I got down to business. At the time of our encounter Tony was in the midst of a late-life comeback. That might sound a little Norma Desmond—FYI, back in the day, Tony had been pals with Gloria Swanson and Greta Garbo, Louella Parsons, Fred Astaire, and Marion Davies, amongst others—but fashion brands and mags were shooting ad campaigns in his fantasy garden and his even more fantastical interior. Tony, and his creative partner Hutton Wilkinson were looking for a retail partner to sell Tony's gargantuan maximalist necklaces. I was hoping that Barneys department store in New York, my employer, might seal the deal. These massive collars called to mind the kind of adornment worn by Maria Montez or Anne Baxter in an old epic movie. They were histrionic and theatrical and the opposite of what was being sold at Zales a couple of miles away at the Beverly Center.

Tony and I discussed the possibility, fingers crossed, of exhibiting his work at the Barneys glam palace on Wilshire Boulevard. We would invite all the LA groovers—Lisa Eisner, Liz Goldwyn, Annie and Tim Street-Porter, Kelly Lynch, Anjelica Huston, Tracee Ellis Ross—to come buy jewelry and kiss those rings. As we discussed the details of a potential event, I could clearly see Tony glazing over. Maximalists are not known for their willingness to tackle minutiae.

When it came time to leave, Tony clutched my hand in his beringed grip: 'Phone me. I will give you a decision by the end of the week.' I tried to imagine where the Duquette telephone might be located. Most likely malachite faux-finished and stuffed in a broom cupboard. I flashed on a memory of visiting David Hicks' maxi-pad in Albany, the legendary London apartment building Terence Stamp and Fleur Cowles once called home. Hick's widow, Lady Pamela Mountbatten, proudly announced that her legendary maximalist decorator hubby had long since eliminated their kitchen. The couple's tea-making needs were supplied by an electric kettle, which was stashed under a hallway statue, inside the pedestal. 'If Fortnum's was closed, we would boil an egg inside the kettle,' admitted Lady Pamela. Maximalists take great pleasure in secreting mundane household appliances.

As instructed, I waited till the end of the week and then made the call to Dawnridge. I was praying that nobody from Nieman Marcus or Saks had beaten me to it, and that we, Barneys, might become Tony's sole collaborator.

'Yes, I would love to present my jewelry at Barneys!'

Sheesh.

Relief was followed by horror when Tony announced his one stipulation: 'You must flood the main floor of the store with water and turn it into a lagoon. I want my jewelry displayed on floating lily pads. Real not fake.' Was he joking? Of course he wasn't.

Tony Duquette was a maximalist, and maximalists are not concerned with health and safety codes. It would never occur to a maximalist to worry about the destruction and death—'Fashionable Hordes Electrocuted at Cocktail Party!'—that might ensue when you flood the floor of a department store with H_2O. A maximalist would never fret about the blown fuses, the mold, and the mayhem which might result from redirecting the Colorado River—LA's most precious resource—into the interior of an eighty thousand square foot store for a meet-the-designer fete.

Have I made my point? The true maximalist, in addition to being a visionary, is also fabulously uncompromising. As a result, maximalism has always left a trail of tassels and tears.

The history of maximalism is entwined with tyranny and imperialism. Those Egyptian pyramids did not build themselves. And while we are in that region, let's talk about those royal tombs. Regarding impulsive spending in her later years, my gran always used to say, 'Treat yourself! After all, you can't take it with you.' The Egyptians made a mockery of gran's adage. After living lives of festooned fabulosity, the Egyptian royals bedded down surrounded by, not a few, but all of their favorite things.

The Greeks were more restrained and minimal—chic white draperies and architectural symmetry wherever possible—preferring to enhance their lives with philosophical introspections. The conquering Romans quickly put an end to Greek understatement. As Voltaire so aptly put it, 'The ancient Romans built their greatest masterpieces of architecture, their amphitheaters, for wild beasts to fight in.'

After watching young lads gored by wild boars and lions, the Romans retreated to their palatial cribs which were adorned with flaming braziers, mosaics, murals, nifty water features, and reclining couches. Come dinner time, they unleashed gag-inducing banquets—remember those steaming mounds of exotic organ meat in the movie *Fellini Satyricon*?—and orgiastic sexual displays. I'm talking to you, Caligula, and you too Heliogabalus. Naughty! Emperor Nero was even worse: when he required ambient light at his bacchanals, he commissioned burning Christians. Who needs dimmer switches when you've got the subtle glow of carbonizing flesh?

The Dark Ages, let's be honest, was a less-than-fascinating time for décor of any description. It's not surprising that no shelter magazines survive from this period. Yes, the printing press had yet to be invented, but even if it had, the harried population was too focused on basic needs like gathering firewood and trying not to be eaten by wolves or pillaged by tall blonde Vikings to bother reading about whether their pillows should be chopped or plumped.

The Renaissance saw trade routes extend far and wide, bringing sumptuous wares to aristocrats and the newly rich. As a result, exhibitionist décor kicked off. In the coming centuries the spoils of colonialism and the wealth of the Industrial Revolution fueled this impulse toward showing off. Don't knock it. Showing off is a basic human impulse. Without it, the book you are holding in your hot little hands, would not exist.

The mega wealth of the Victorian Age produced explosions of showy-offy interior design on both sides of the Atlantic. The old order crumbled, and a new ambitious class—paging Henry James and Edith Wharton—festooned their pads with swags, stuffed peacocks, side-tables, end tables, tea tables, each groaning with porcelain bibelots, tortoise-shell gewgaws, and silver thingies. Dingle-ball fringe dangled from every fireplace, lampshade, swag, and bustle. Shares in dingle-balls surged.

This orgy of *fin-de-siècle* szhoosh finds its patron saint in Dorian Gray, Oscar Wilde's fictional creation. Dorian's descent into hell is paralleled by his addiction to décor and to the accumulation of … you name it, and Dor accumulated it. At night he frequents opium dens and dockside brothels, and during the day, he fills his house with textiles, jewels, musical instruments, ecclesiastical costumery, and 'symphonic arrangements of exotic flowers.' Wilde's character forges the template for the flea-market queens who bustle through Clignancourt in Paris and Alfies in London to this very day, quite possibly after an exhausting night at a dockside brothel or the contemporary equivalent.

Dorian draws inspiration and justification from the maximalist excess of history: 'How exquisite life had once been! How gorgeous in its pomp and decoration! Even to read of the luxury of the dead was wonderful.' This is a common maximalist trait: justifying costly new splendors with vague historical references. Ludwig of Bavaria did it, so why can't I?!

So Dorian Gray looked backward. If he had looked forward, he would have seen—most likely with horror because he was a snobby little bitch—the explosive, mega-democratization of maximalism that now characterizes our age. Maximalism for everyone!

The twentieth century was a time of great wars, social change, and—drumroll!—gob-smackingly great design. Yes, I know that this is the century that produced Beanie Babies, pole-dancing, and child pageants, but it is also—another drumroll!—the period that birthed the iconic genres and sensibilities that cumulatively define what we think of as interior design. Chronologically, we are talking Art Nouveau, Arts and Crafts, Art Deco, Futurism, Mid-Century Modernism, and Brutalism.

This unfurling sequence of styles—the foundations of contemporary interior design—followed a fairly logical progression, until it didn't. Permit me to explain: This trajectory has an action-reaction cadence. Swirly natural William Morris prints were followed by machine-age Art Deco geometry. Plump squishy furniture was succeeded by angular stuff with spindly legs. The maxi followed the mini. Uptight narrow neckties were followed by wide sleazy geezer styles. Twee conventional restraint was eclipsed by smelly bohemian *dégagé*. Tarted-up supermodels are succeeded by scrubbed waifs. Action and reaction. Geddit? Repeat after me: Action. Reaction.

This system holds tight until the final decades of the twentieth century, and the arrival of—one more drumroll, and then I promise I'll stop before you get a headache—the postmodern era. Postmodernism is characterized by mashing and sampling, high-low, camp, a love of pastiche, and a willful lack of seriousness. Yes, we are talking about the aesthetic free-for-all which began in the 1980s. (The seeds were sown in the groovy Warhol 60s when Brillo boxes became ART.) This is the period when culture, instead of generating newness, starts to mine itself for inspiration. The soundtrack for this new movement is the 1987 Love and Rockets song 'No New Tales to Tell'. Henceforth the only way to tell a new tale is to graze upon everything that has gone prior and then slice and dice it in the Cuisinart.

The rules-out-the-window aspect of postmodernism triggered an explosion of maximalism, characterized by infantile bright colors and wacky juxtapositions. In design we are talking Memphis and Frank Gehry. Also consider the work of Robert Venturi, who famously morphed Mies van der Rohe's 'less is more' edict into 'less is a bore.'

Postmodernism impacted all aspects of culture. I'm thinking of Vanilla Ice and MC Hammer, popstars who created a new tale by adding one note to a preexisting number and then calling the result their own, with enormous panache, I might add. In fashion I would cite maximalist *de la mode*, Jean Paul Gaultier, in particular his stage costumes for Madonna, most notably the zoot-suit cone-bra monocle period. The impact of this new sensibility on interior design was KAPOW. Postmodernism lit the fuse and opened the door to décor without borders, a glorious maximalist goulash where all styles and combos thereof are currently on the menu, often in the same dish.

Postmodernism led to the divine diversity that we have today, where all styles are, as previously stated, concurrently available. Your house may be bohemian Big Sur, but your neighbor's is high-voltage hedge-fund glamour, and his neighbor is an art-collecting rapper whose crib is Tik-Tok ready. We now live in the era of you do you. Or maybe, your decorator does you. Either way, unhinged personal expression is king/queen.

But wait. There's more….

It's a shame Tony Duquette did not live long enough to witness the rise of the metaverse. Those looking for something truly deranged and excessive can head to the metaverse and drop some Bitcoin on an NFT of a starchitect-designed villa. Being *d'un certain âge*, I am not entirely sure what any of that last sentence means.

But before you head to the barricades to protest income inequality, let me offer you some reassurance: maximalism is no longer just about dough. In parallel with the glam palaces of the rich, a new generation of outsiders is creating sensational interiors using yard-sale furniture and Duquette-ian techniques that were more often found in window displays: decoupage, upcycling, hacking, collage, badinage, and lots of paint. Throw your glue gun into your wheelie, check in to Trixie Mattel's Trixie Motel, and celebrate the democratization of maximalism.

As you peruse the high/low maximal majesty of this glorious tome, you will inevitably ask yourself, What, on Earth, is the motherluvin' point of it all? Why, in this age of enlightenment, do we continue to show off in such as specific manner. *Pourquoi*?

Here's the deal: Décor, when taken to extremes, is both fabulously pointless and wildly justified. Andy Warhol once described himself as 'deeply superficial.' The same can be said of maximalism. It is a world of surfaces and appearances, underpinned by profundity and positivity.

Let's start with the most obvious: maximalism is a positive force because it fosters artisanal creativity. Just as the *petites mains* of the Paris couture salons—the craftspeople whose skills realize the couturier's vision—are able to maintain and develop their crafts (and pay their rent), so it is with the artisans of maxi décor. The weavers, furniture-makers, tile-makers, tassel-makers, shade-makers, beaders, embroiderers, upholsterers, muralists, and decorative finishers are sustained, creatively and financially, by the propulsive energy of unhinged maximalism. And let's not forget the architects, builders, plumbers, electricians, and that whole crew. #jobcreation

Maximalism is now accessible to all via social media, where it has found a perfect home. Your Insta fans the flames of exhibitionist décor and spews images to a global audience. Yes, I know I said maximalists were wicked people who were intent on having their rings kissed and intimidating spectators, but I'm prone to exaggeration. As per Diana Vreeland, 'exaggeration is my only reality.' (When Vreeland, a high priestess of maximalist thought, famously commanded her decorator Billy Baldwin to turn her living room into 'a garden from hell,' she wasn't kidding.)

Images of creative fabulosity can produce FOMO in certain individuals—if this is you, then please seek professional help—but most of us, with our scrolling and swiping, get a positive charge from viewing maxi décor. I personally find maximalism to be life-enhancing and entertaining, and I am continually impressed by the effort and imagination on display.

Thanks to my husbear Jonathan Adler I have inhabited various maximalist aeries and bolt holes and can attest to the psychological benefits. When I wake up in that massive chrome vintage Paul Evans brutalist four-poster bed, I am filled with a sense of optimism and possibility. Thought bubble: the next time we have a cocktail party, we should flood this room and serve hors d'oeuvres on giant lily pads. Why the hell not?

Without show-offs and maximalists, the world would be at the mercy of minimalists—*quelle horreur*!—and this book would not exist. As per Robert Venturi, 'less is a bore.' The desire to go over the top is the gasoline which powers the decorating business. And you minimalists, less of the disdain please. You should never look down on maximalists. You need maximalists. You need the counterpoint. Without the exuberance and excess of maximalism, you have no *raison d'être*. And here's the kicker: the reverse is not true. Maximalism needs no greige or beige minimalist opposition to justify its existence. Maximalism is too big to fail.

EXCESS AND EXUBERANCE

Is a book on maximalism in decoration necessary? We very much think so. Maximalism is sheer and unadulterated joy. And joy, in today's too often brutal world, is as rare as free diamonds. Yes, maximalism is everywhere of late, cheered and celebrated in the shelter magazines and online by design aficionados, but its traditions and signifiers are as old as the pyramids.

This inspirational collection of more than two-hundred residential interiors draws from a long and illustrious history of maximalism that transcends time and geography. It brings together the many and varied ways that maximalism can be expressed in interiors, making the point that maximalism is not about following aesthetic rules, it's as much about attitude as it is about style. It also proves that maximalism has been with us, in one guise or another, for more than four hundred years. The earliest maximalist interiors you'll find here date from the 1600s and include (of course) the ground zero of maximalism, the Palace of Versailles. Then from the next several centuries, we have some of the most extraordinary castles, palazzi, schlosses, châteaux, dachas, and villas from across Europe, and North America—and beyond.

But let's not forget the twentieth century, which is when things get really controversial. The work of some of the doyennes of decorating—Ann Getty, Billy Haines, Dorothy Draper, and Elsie de Wolfe—are reappraised and feature here among the hallowed ranks of the maximalists. And bringing things right up to the minute we have an explosion of maximalist talent from contemporary designers, including Thomas Britt, Peter Marino, India Mahdavi, Miles Redd, Jonathan Adler, and Justina Blakeney.

Rich, poor, simple, complex, old or new, found or custom-made, there are more ways to be maximal than any set of decorating rules can possibly account for. It is mysterious and miraculous and can be found in innumerable guises. But some recurrent tropes that can be spotted among these pages include the bombastic use of colors, patterns, prints, tapestries, sequins, ruffles, fringes, rugs, pillows, cushions, canopies, gilt-edged everything, layer upon layer of art, and *objet*, swags of fabric on every viable surface, not to mention a whole safari's worth of leopard, tiger, and zebra motifs. Always more. Never less.

What the interiors in this book have in common beyond their physical characteristics though, is a discernible warmth, a sense of humor, and a willingness to bring drama into the realms of everyday life—all brought together within the container of four walls, a floor, and a ceiling. But beware, these interiors elicit strong emotions—awe, shock, and delight among them. You may even find spaces here that are thrilling, appalling, loud, louche, fun, humorous, sophisticated, vulgar, or just plain unashamedly joyful!

Welcome to our book, Maximalism, and it's a wild party! Behold maximalism and experience the joy, the excess, and the exuberance!

Michela Goldschmied ◆ Asolo Residence, Living, and Dining Area ◆ Asolo, Veneto, Italy ◆ 2018

John Nash ◆ Buckingham Palace, White Drawing Room ◆ London, England, UK ◆ 1820

Tom Scheerer ♦ Lyford Cay Club House, Main Drawing Room ♦ Nassau, New Providence, Bahamas ♦ 2011

Ann Getty with Parish-Hadley ◆ Pacific Heights Residence, Sitting Room ◆ San Francisco, California, USA ◆ 1979

Jacques Garcia ◆ Château du Champ de Bataille, Cabinet of Curiosities ◆ Eure, Normandy, France ◆ 1990

Eva Cavalli ◆ Eva Cavalli Home, Living Room ◆ Florence, Tuscany, Italy ◆ 2018

Robert Couturier ◆ New York City Residence, Home Office ◆ New York City, New York, USA ◆ 2011

Rudolf Nureyev • Paris Apartment, Dining Room • Paris, France • 1985

Guérard Family ◆ Les Prés d'Eugénie, Empress Aisle Salon ◆ Eugénie-les-Bains, Nouvelle-Aquitaine, France ◆ 2009

Nick Olsen ◆ Brooklyn Townhouse, Living Room ◆ Brooklyn, New York, USA ◆ 2013

Jules Hardouin-Mansart for Louis XIV • Palace of Versailles, War Room • Versailles, Île-de-France, France • 1686

Nikolaus Pacassi for Maria Theresa, Ruler of the Habsburg Empire ◆ Castle Schönbrunn, Napoleon Room ◆ Vienna, Austria ◆ 1765

Gianni Versace ◆ Casa Casuarina, Bedroom ◆ Miami, Florida, USA ◆ 1990

Denning & Fourcade • New York Apartment, Sitting Room • New York City, New York, USA • 1995

Valerian Rybar and Jean-François Daigre ◆ Paris House, Salon ◆ Paris, France ◆ 1989

Christophe Huet • Château de Chantilly, Grand Singerie • Chantilly, Hauts-de-France, France • 1737

Francesca DiMattio ◆ Manhattan Townhouse, Living Room ◆ New York City, New York, USA ◆ 2022

Maharaja Sawai Jai Singh II • Jaipur City Palace, Chandra Mahal, Shobha Niwas (Hall of Beauty) • Jaipur, Rajasthan, India • 1727

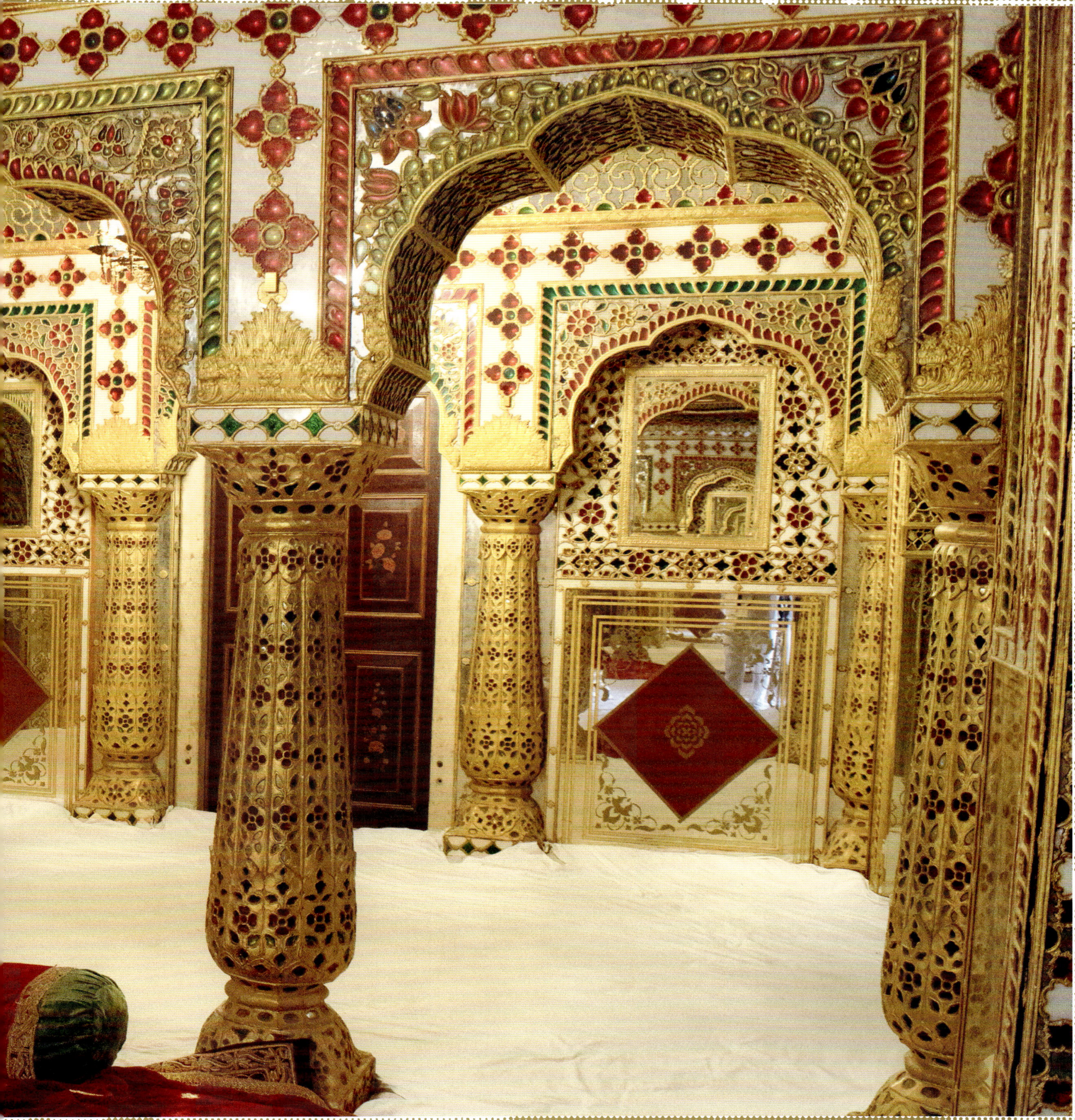

Henri Samuel for Susan Gutfreund ♦ Fifth Avenue Apartment, Living Room ♦ New York City, New York, USA ♦ 1987

39

Tony Duquette and Hutton Wilkinson ♦ Dawnridge, Garden Room ♦ Beverly Hills, California, USA ♦ 1955

Billy Baldwin for Diana Vreeland ◆ Park Avenue Apartment, Living Room ◆ New York City, New York, USA ◆ 1955

Mario Buatta ◆ Aileen Mehle Residence, Dining Room ◆ New York City, New York, USA ◆ 2011

43

Ann Getty • Getty Residence, Sitting Room • San Francisco, California, USA • 1987

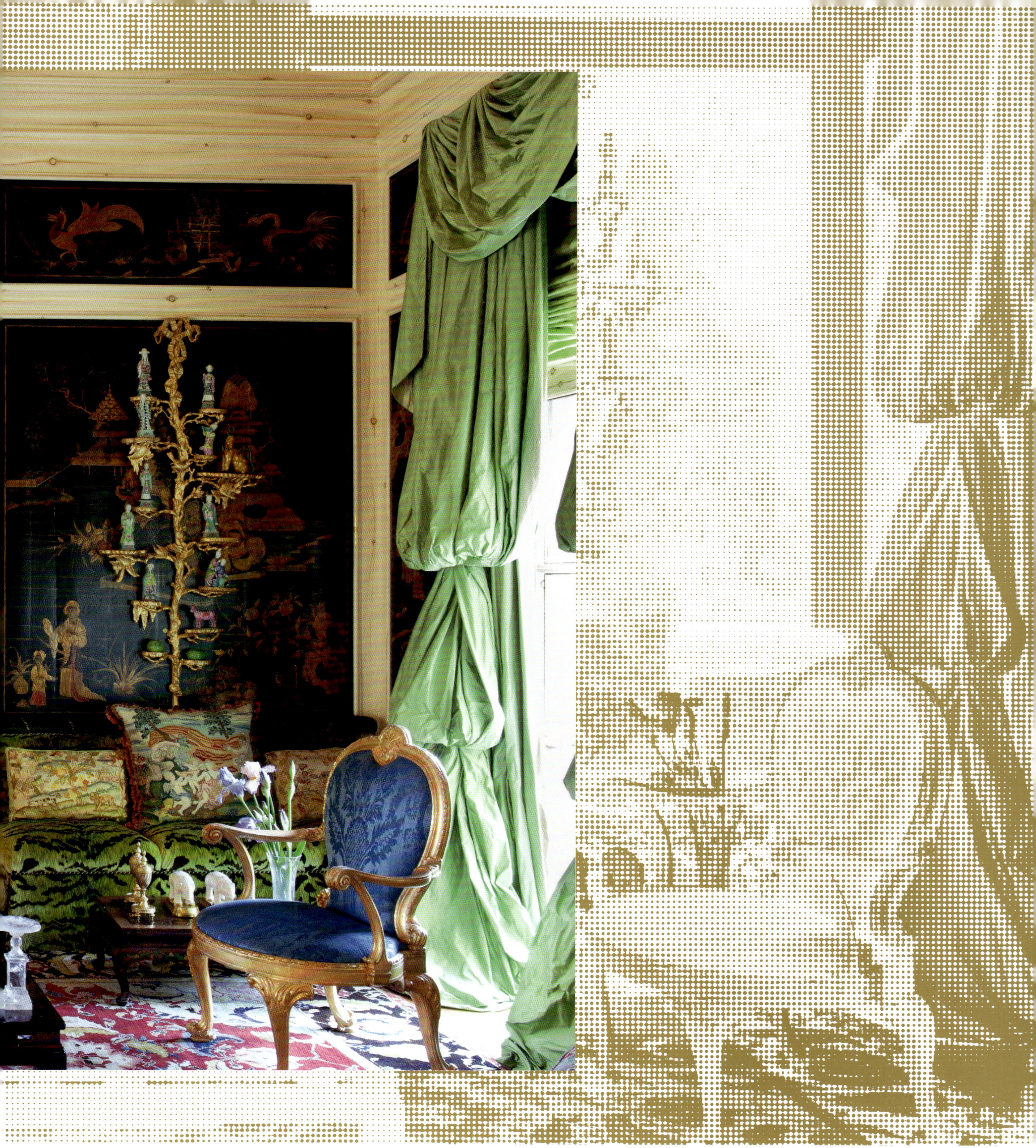

Justina Blakeney • Southern California Home, Main Bedroom • California, USA • 2022

Ashley Hicks • The Albany, Living Room • London, England, UK • 2017

Anthony Baratta • Baratta Apartment, Living Room • Miami, Florida, USA • 2008

Vladimir Kagan ◆ Kagan Apartment, Living Room ◆ New York City, New York, USA ◆ 2015

Joseph Holzman • Joseph Holtzman Installation • New York City, New York, USA • 2020

Dorothy Draper ◆ Greenbrier Hotel, Presidential Suite ◆ White Sulphur Springs, West Virginia, USA ◆ 1948

Jorge Pardo ◆ Reyes Residence, Kitchen and Sitting Area ◆ Playa De Naguabo, Puerto Rico ◆ 2006

Rose Anne de Pampelonne ◆ Paris Apartment, Living Room ◆ Paris, France ◆ 2008

ALWAYS LEAVE THEM WANTING LESS.

ANDY WARHOL

Celerie Kemble and Lindsey Herod ◆ Houston Home, Living Room ◆ Houston, Texas, USA ◆ 2016

57

Dorothy Draper • Greenbrier Hotel, Presidential Suite • White Sulphur Springs, West Virginia, USA • 1948

Elsie de Wolfe ◆ Planting Fields Foundation, Tea House ◆ Oyster Bay, New York, USA ◆ 1915

Job Smeets • Studio Job Headquarters, Bedroom and Ensuite • Antwerp, Belgium • 2018

Elvis Presley ◆ Graceland, TV Room ◆ Memphis, Tennessee, USA ◆ 1974

Elvis Presley • Graceland, Music Room • Memphis, Tennessee, USA • 1974

Sasha Bikoff ◆ Kips Bay Showhouse, Staircase ◆ New York City, New York, USA ◆ 2018

Amanda Nisbet Design • Nisbet Residence, Living Room • New York City, New York, USA • 2017

Alisha Gwen ◆ Private Residence, Living Room ◆ Gibsonia, Pennsylvania, USA ◆ 2016

Bradford Shellhammer ◆ Summer House, Living Room, and Bar ◆ Orange County, New York, USA ◆ 2012

Roger de Cabrol • East Village Loft, Living Room • New York City, New York, USA • 2014

King Louis XIV • Château de Chambord, Ceremonial Bedroom of Louis XIV • Chambord, Centre-Val de Loire, France • 1680

Alidad ◆ Kuwait Residence, Sitting Room ◆ Kuwait City, Kuwait ◆ 2012

Brett Leemkuil • Queens Apartment, Sleeping Area • Queens, New York, USA • 2015

71

Jacques Garcia ♦ Château du Champ de Bataille, Apollo Salon ♦ Eure, Normandy, France ♦ 1990

Oberto Gili • Farmhouse, Bedroom • Turin, Piedmont, Italy • 2017

James Deering and Paul Chalfin ◆ Villa Vizcaya, Bedroom ◆ Miami, Florida, USA ◆ 1922

Ludwig II of Bavaria ◆ Neuschwanstein Castle, Bedroom ◆ Hohenschwangau, Bavaria, Germany ◆ 1884

Tony Duquette and Hutton Wilkinson ◆ Dawnridge, Drawing Room ◆ Beverly Hills, California, USA ◆ 1955

James Aguiar ♦ Brooklyn Apartment, Sitting Room ♦ Brooklyn, New York, USA ♦ 2017

Iris Apfel ◆ Apfel Residence, Sitting Room ◆ New York City, New York, USA ◆ 1978

House of Hackney • Trematon Castle, Flora Delanica Bedroom • Saltash, Cornwall, England, UK • 2021

Mario Buatta • Patricia Altschul Residence, Dining Room • New York City, New York, USA • 2007

Elvis Presley ◆ Graceland, Jungle Room ◆ Memphis, Tennesee, USA ◆ 1974

Robert Kime ◆ South Wraxall Manor, Drawing Room ◆ South Wraxall, Wiltshire, England, UK ◆ 2007

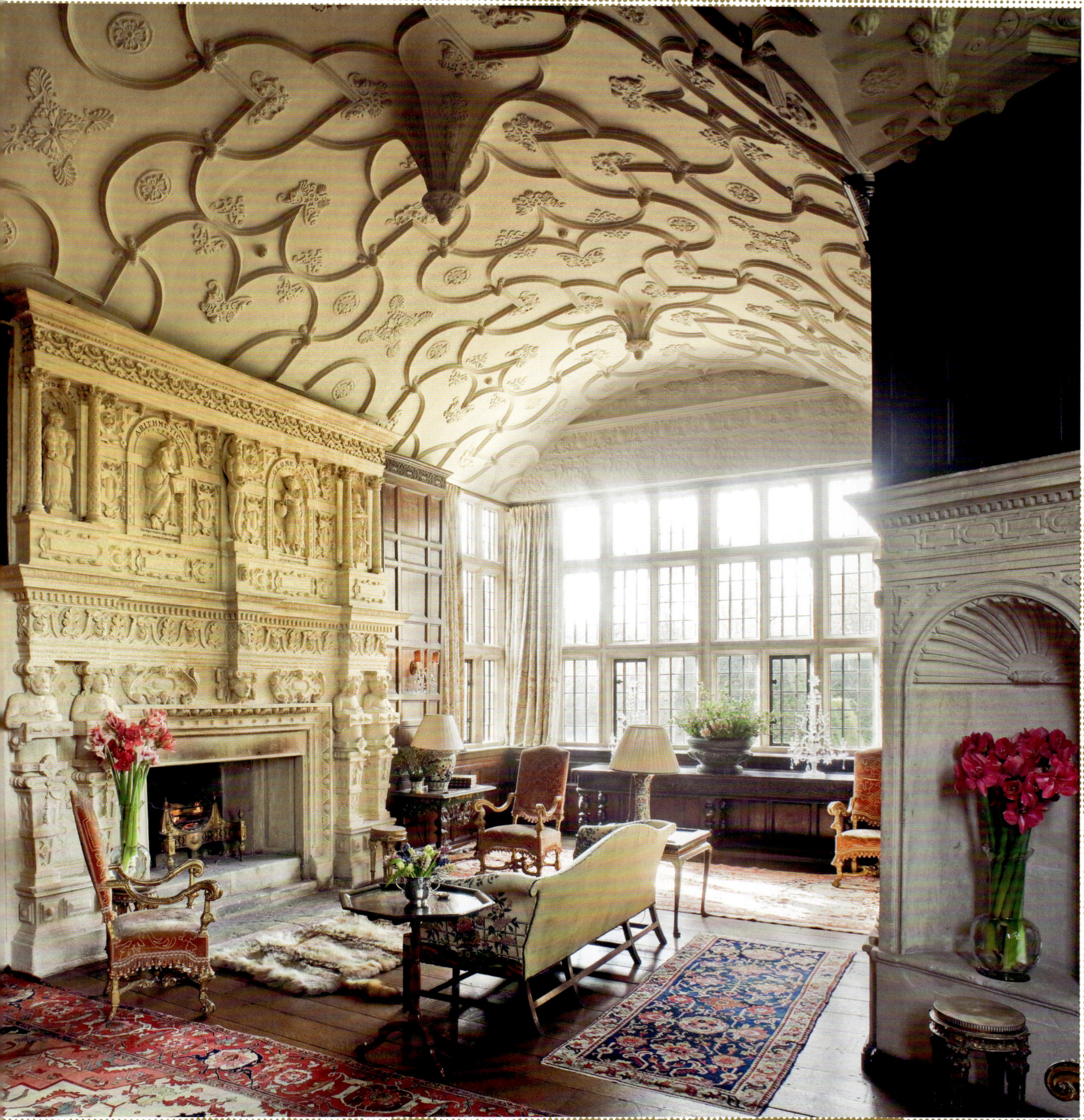

Rudolf Nureyev ◆ Paris Apartment, Living Room ◆ Paris, France ◆ 1985

Donatella Versace • Versace Apartment, Dining Room • Milan, Lombardy, Italy • 1994

85

IF ANYONE TELLS YOU YOUR HAIR IS TOO BIG, GET RID OF THEM. YOU DON'T NEED THAT KIND OF NEGATIVITY IN YOUR LIFE.

DOLLY PARTON

Jules Hardouin-Mansart ♦ Trianon Palace, Salon des Glaces ♦ Versailles, Île-de-France, France ♦ 1687

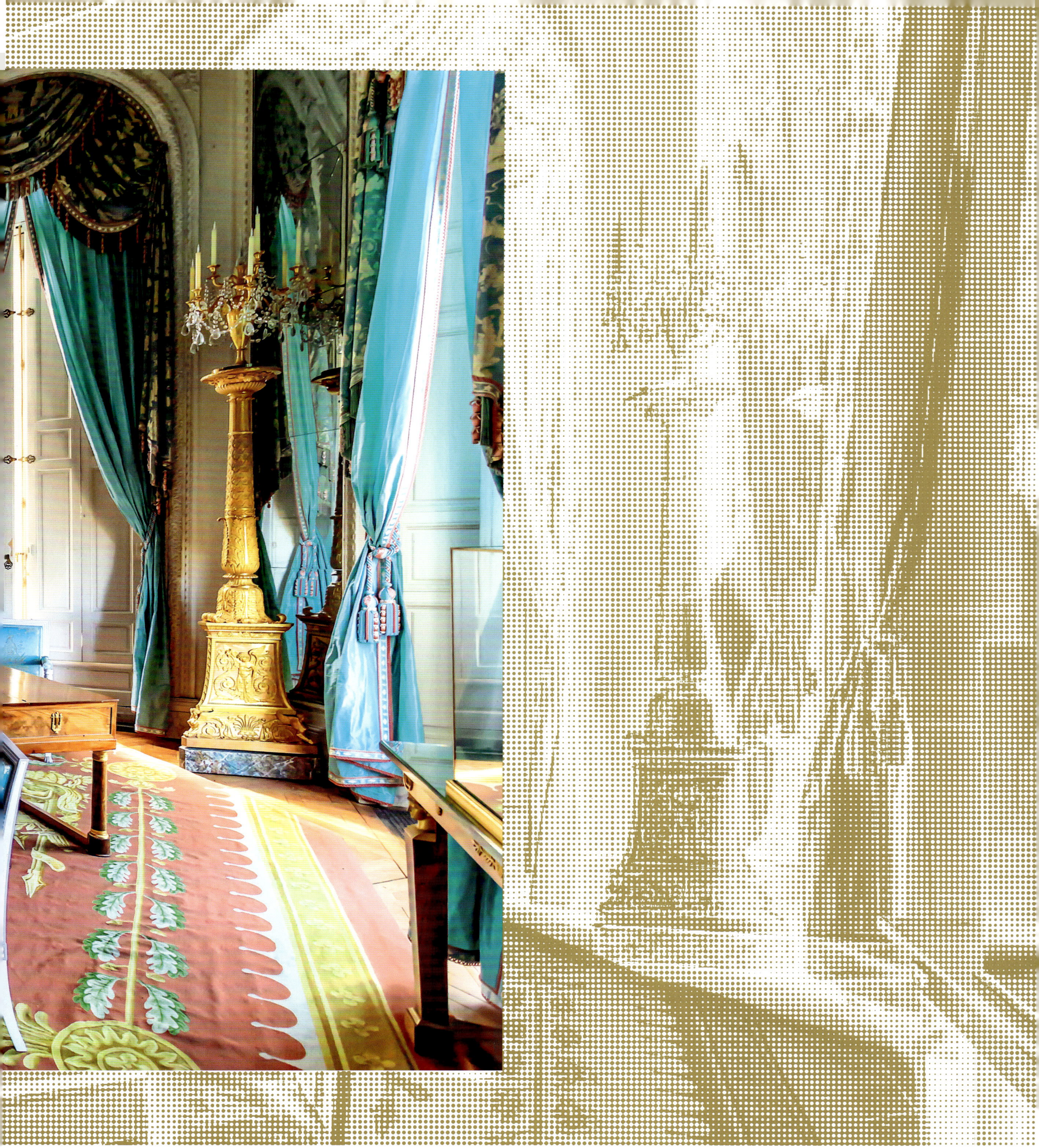

Lapo Elkann ◆ Milan Residence, Living Room ◆ Milan, Lombardy, Italy ◆ 2015

Grisanti & Cussen ◆ Grisanti Residence, Living Room ◆ Santiago, Chile ◆ 2021

Mattia Bonetti ◆ Hong Kong Apartment, Dining Room ◆ Hong Kong, China ◆ 2016

Teo Leo Galerie ◆ Laurent di Benedetto Residence, Living Room ◆ Paris, France ◆ 2022

Sultan Osman III • Topkapi Palace, Imperial Hall • Istanbul, Turkey • 1666

Dita Von Teese ◆ Von Teese Residence, Dining Room ◆ Los Angeles, California, USA ◆ 2018

Lluís Domènech i Montaner • Casa Navàs, Vestibule • Reus, Catalonia, Spain • 1908

Nicodemus Tessin the Elder & Nicodemus Tessin the Younger ◆ Drottningholm Palace, Porcelain Room ◆ Stockholm, Sweden ◆ 1897

Greg Natale ◆ Barwon River House, Living Room ◆ Melbourne, Victoria, Australia ◆ 2017

Marie-Anne Oudejans ◆ Villa Palladio, Bar Palladio ◆ Jaipur, Rajasthan, India ◆ 2022

Richard Bore for Queen Victoria • London Northwestern Railway, Queen Victoria's Royal Saloon • London, England, UK • 1869

Dani Dazey ◆ Trixie Motel, Atomic Bombshell Room ◆ Palm Springs, California, USA ◆ 2022

102   Martyn Thompson ♦ Martyn Thompson, Studio ♦ New York City, New York, USA ♦ 2014

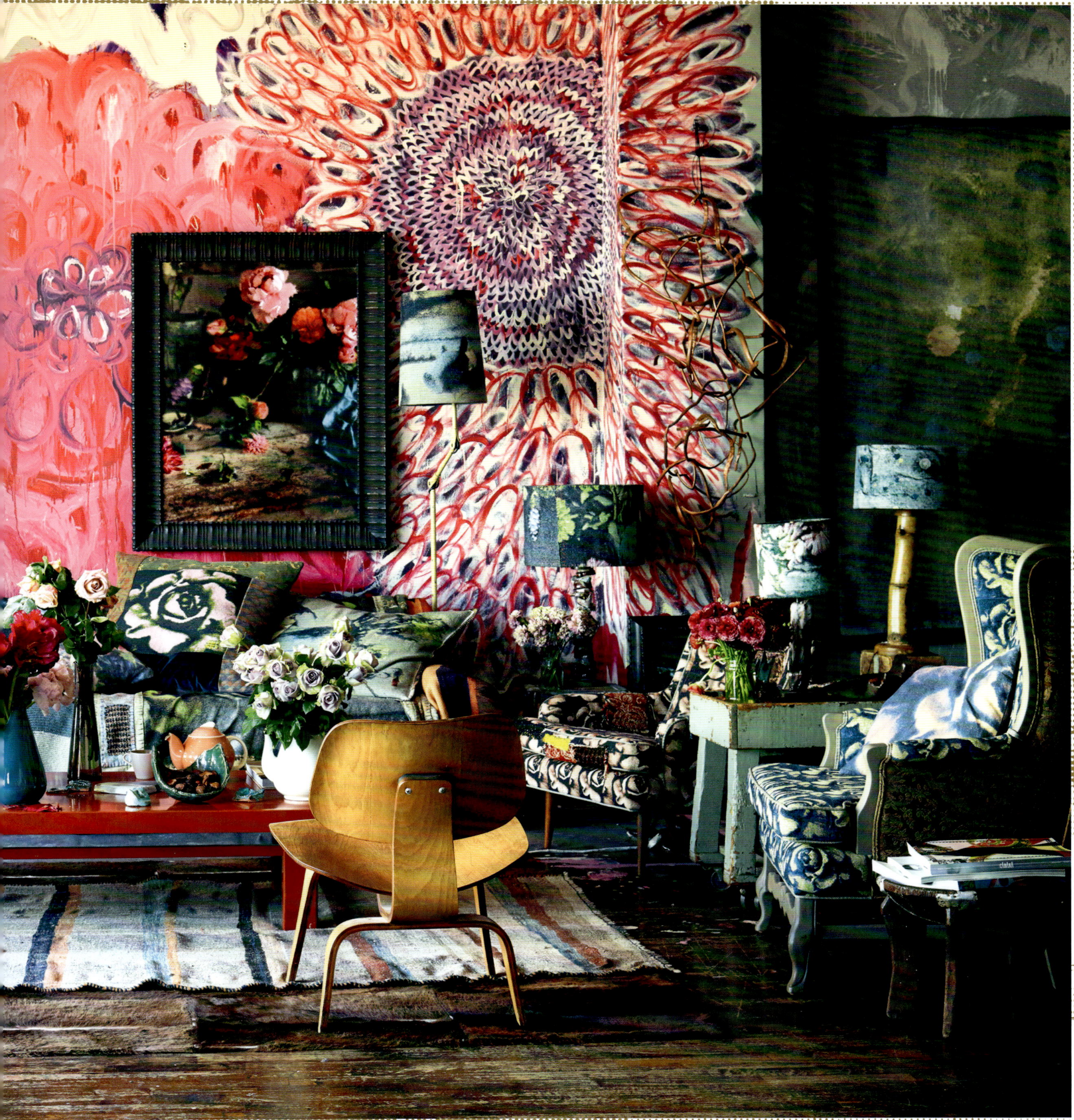

Ann Getty ◆ Getty Residence, Dining Room ◆ San Francisco, California, USA ◆ 1987

Countess Cristiana Brandolini D'Adda • Vistorta, Conservatory • Pordenone, Friuli-Venezia Giulia, Italy • 1972

India Mahdavi ♦ De Gournay Showroom, Private Apartment, Salon ♦ Paris, France ♦ 2020

Sylvester Stallone ◆ Miami House, Living Room ◆ Miami, Florida, USA ◆ 1997

Antti Lovag • Palais Bulles, Living Room • Théoule sur Mer, Provence-Alpes-Côte d'Azur, France • 1980

Anthony Baratta ◆ Pink House, Living Room ◆ New York City, New York, USA ◆ 2015

Denning & Fourcade ◆ Upper East Side Apartment, Library ◆ New York City, New York, USA ◆ 1977

Rouge Absolu ◆ Paris Apartment, Dining Room ◆ Paris, France ◆ 2017

Dani Dazey ◆ Trixie Motel, Pink Flamingo Suite ◆ Palm Springs, California, USA ◆ 2022

Greg Natale ◆ Toorak Penthouse, Dining Room ◆ Melbourne, Victoria, Australia ◆ 2021

House of Hackney ♦ Trematon Castle, Hollyhocks Bedroom ♦ Cornwall, England, UK ♦ 2021

Valentino • Roman Penthouse, Turkish Tent Alcove • Rome, Lazio, Italy • 1970

Sig Bergamin ◆ São Paulo Estate, Living Room ◆ São Paulo, Brazil ◆ 2015

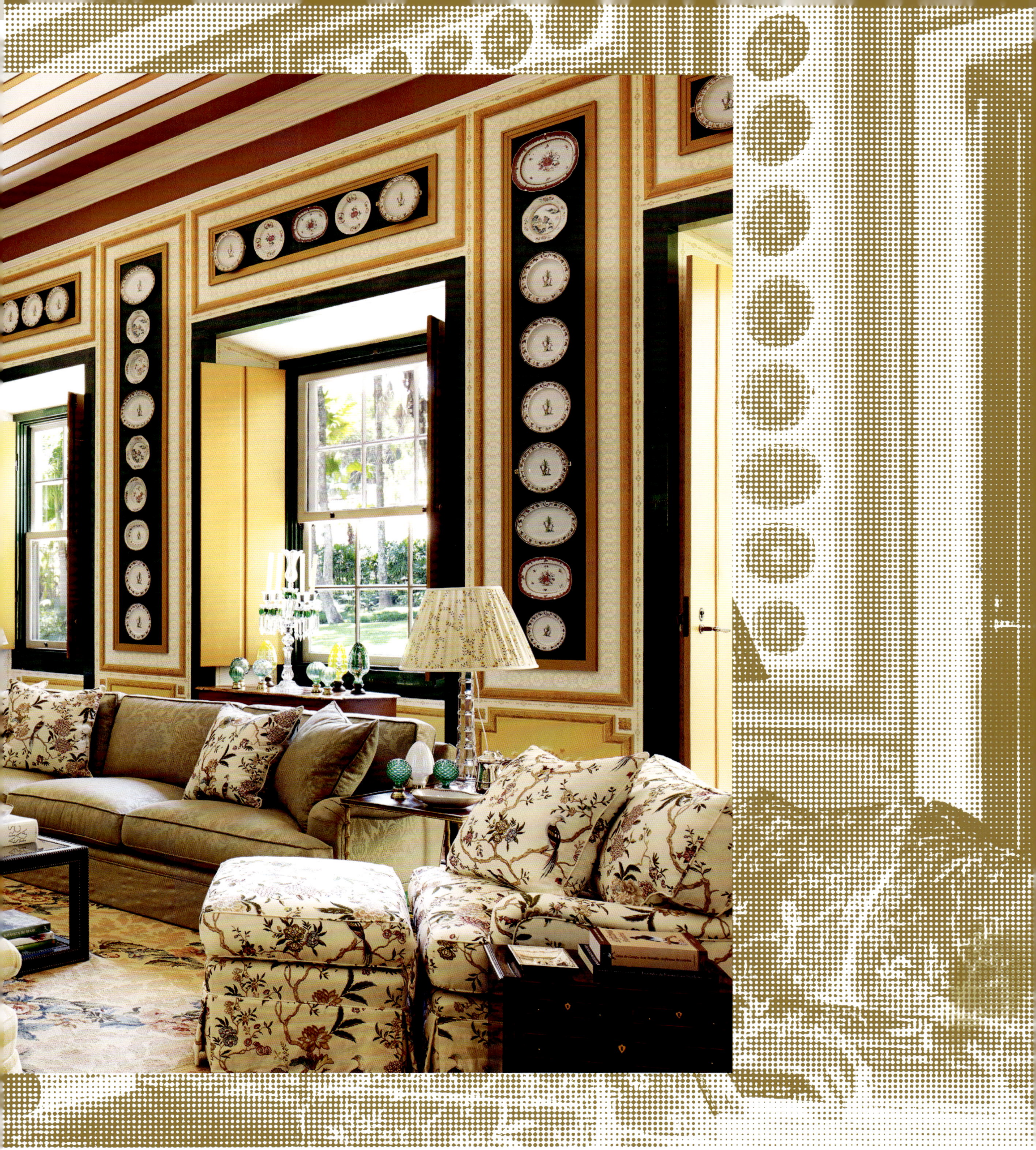

Mario Buatta ◆ Manhattan Apartment, Sitting Room ◆ New York City, New York, USA ◆ 1997

119

Kelly Wearstler • Bellagio Residence, Dressing Room • Los Angeles, California, USA • 2011

Ferdinand II • Pena Palace, Arabic Room • Sintra, Portugal • 1854

Alidad ◆ Parisian Pied-à-Terre, Drawing Room ◆ Paris, France ◆ 2006

Inigo Jones for the Earl of Pembroke ◆ Wilton House, Double Cube Room ◆ Wilton, Wiltshire, England, UK ◆ 1653

Rex Whistler for Sir Philip Sassoon ◆ Port Lympne Mansion, Tent Room ◆ Port Lympne, Kent, England, UK ◆ 1913

Pedro Espírito Santo ◆ Pedro Espírito Santo Residence, Salon ◆ Lisbon, Portugal ◆ 2015

126　　　Peter Marino　◆　Woody House, Living Room　◆　Long Island, New York, USA　◆　2019

Liberace • The Liberace Mansion, Bedroom • Las Vegas, Nevada, USA • 1974

Peter Marino ◆ Woody House, Sitting Room ◆ Long Island, New York, USA ◆ 2019

Jonathan Adler ◆ Jonathan Adler and Simon Doonan's Apartment, Bedroom ◆ New York City, New York, USA ◆ 2018

TEAR DOWN THAT BITCH OF A BEARING WALL AND PUT THAT WINDOW WHERE THE WINDOW OUGHT TO BE.

FAYE DUNAWAY AS JOAN CRAWFORD IN 'MOMMIE DEAREST'.

Eva Cavalli • Eva Cavalli Home, Living Room • Florence, Tuscany, Italy • 2018

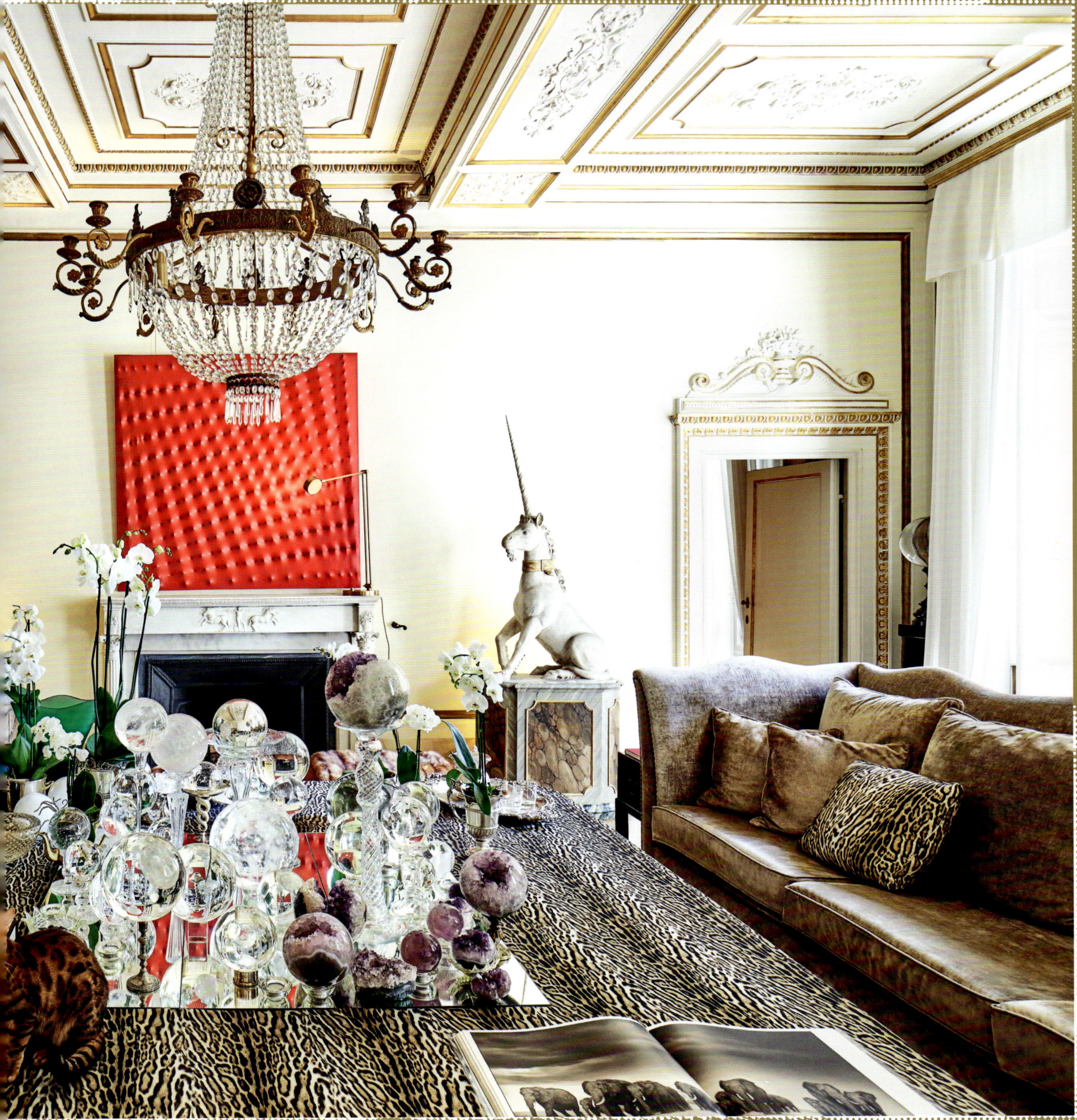

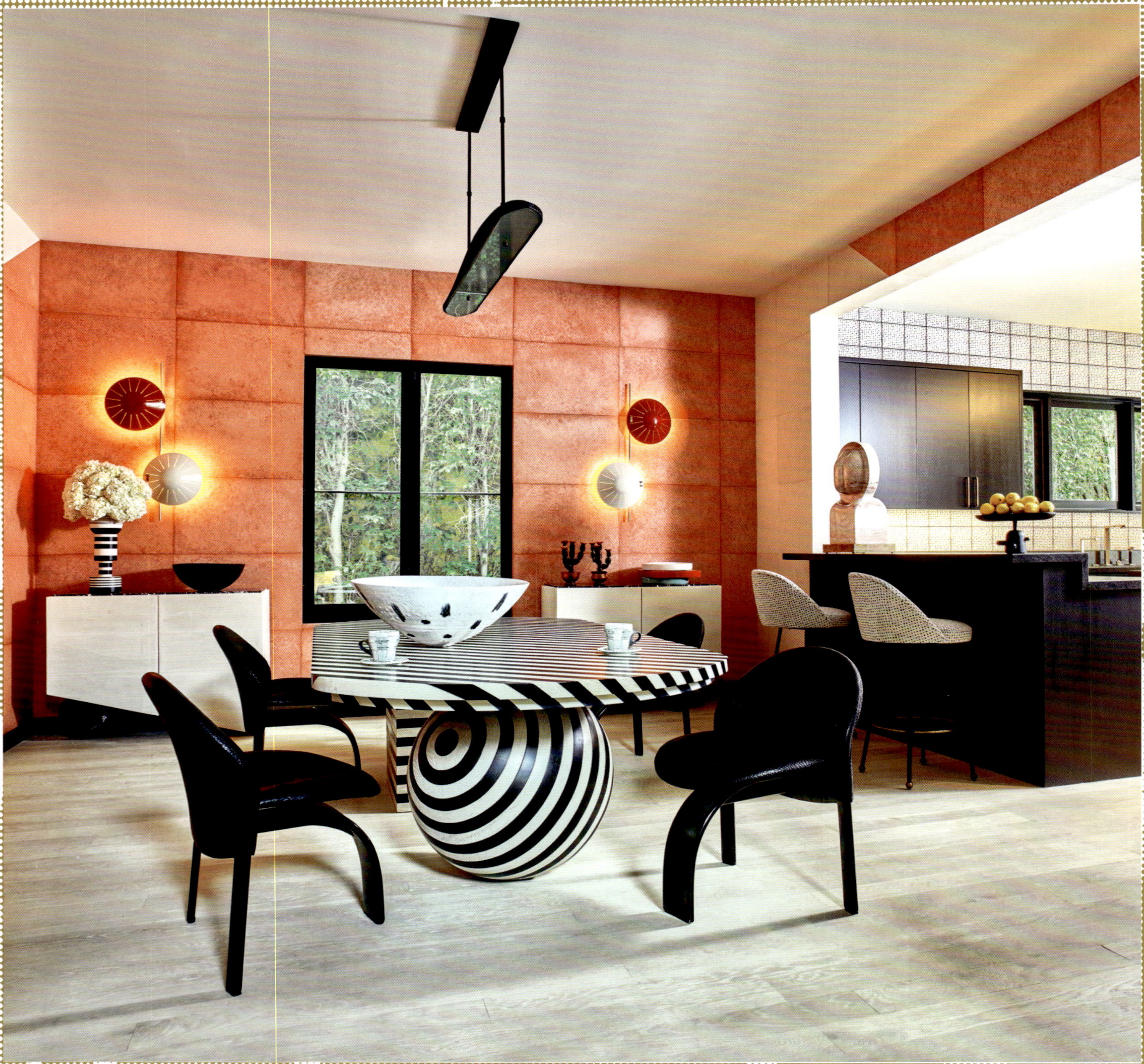

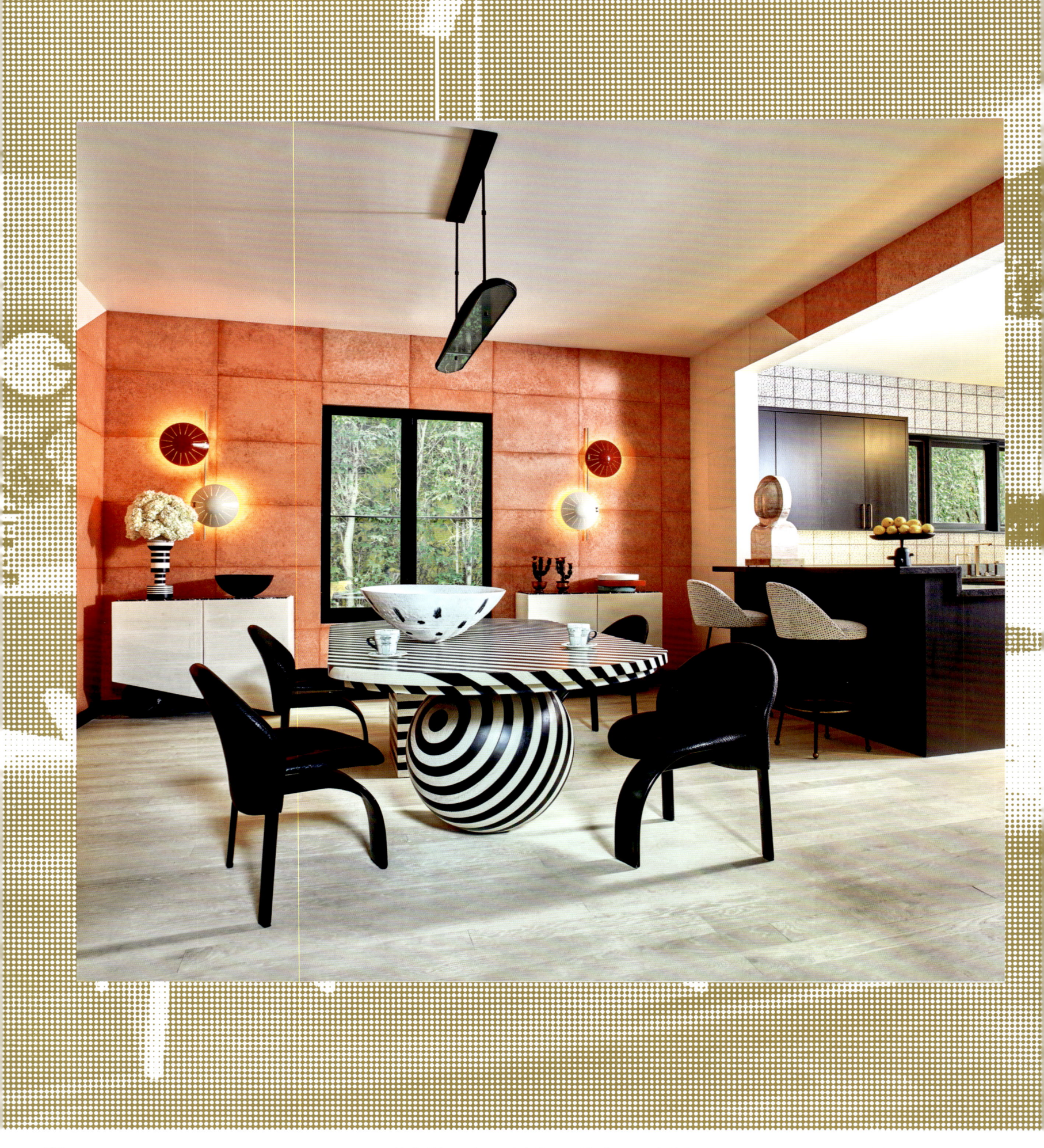

Young Huh Interior Design ◆ Kips Bay Showhouse, Sitting Room ◆ New York City, New York, USA ◆ 2019

135

José de la Cruz Porfirio Díaz Mori • Castillo de Chapultepec, Emperor's Music Room • Mexico City, Mexico • 1864

Alidad ◆ London Townhouse, Salon ◆ London, England, UK ◆ 2008

Baron Ferdinand de Rothschild ◆ Waddesdon Manor, Tower Drawing Room ◆ Location ◆ 1883

Hutton Wilkinson • Malibu Home, Bedroom • Los Angeles, California, USA • 2015

Jacques Garcia • Château du Champ de Bataille, Salon Asiatique • Eure, Normandy, France • 1990

Thomas Britt ◆ Pied-à-Terre, Living Room ◆ San Francisco, California, USA ◆ 2013

Jimmy Jamieson and Susan Barrett ◆ St. Louis Guest House, Drawing Room ◆ St. Louis, Missouri, USA ◆ 2020

Michelle Nussbaumer ◆ Nussbaumer Residence, Living Room ◆ Dallas, Texas, USA ◆ 2020

144   Dorothy Draper ◆ Greenbrier Hotel, Lobby ◆ White Sulphur Springs, West Virginia, USA ◆ 1948

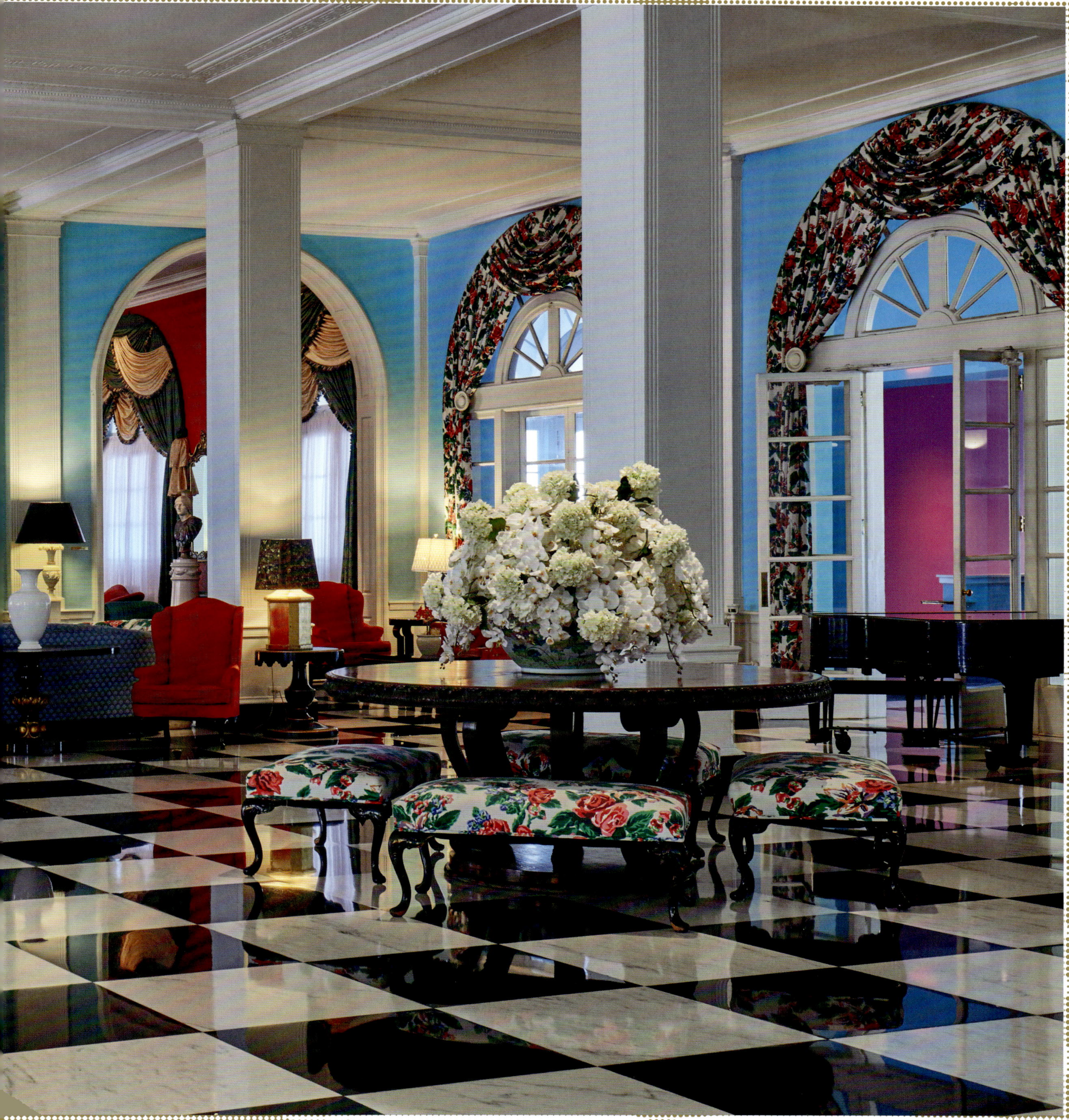

Gianni Versace • Casa Casuarina, Bedroom • Miami, Florida, USA • 1990

Alidad • Mayfair Pied-à-Terre, Sitting Room • London, England, UK • 2012

Sheldon Harte • San Francisco House, Dining Room • San Francisco, California, USA • 2015

Emilio Terry and Carlos de Beistegui ◆ Château de Groussay, Tartar Tent ◆ Montfort-l'Amaury, Île-de-France, France ◆ 1963

Kelly Wearstler • Bel Air Mansion, Living Room • Los Angeles, California, USA • 2012

Tony Duquette and Hutton Wilkinson • Wilshire Corridor Penthouse, Sitting Area • Los Angeles, California, USA • 2020

Maryam Mahdavi ◆ Paris Apartment, Sitting Area ◆ Paris, France ◆ 2020

Alberto Pinto ◆ Paris Apartment, Living Room ◆ Paris, France ◆ 2019

Michelle Nussbaumer ◆ Hacienda Buena Fe, Bedroom ◆ San Miguel de Allende, Guanajuato, Mexico ◆ 2019

Elvis Presley • Graceland, Bedroom • Memphis, Tennessee, USA • 1965

Sir James Thornhill • Old Royal Naval College, Painted Hall • London, England, UK • 1726

157

EXAGGERATION IS MY ONLY REALITY.

DIANA VREELAND

Alidad ◆ Kuwait Residence, Library ◆ Kuwait City, Kuwait ◆ 2012

161

Antoni Gaudí • Casa Vicens, Smoking Room • Barcelona, Catalonia, Spain • 1885

Haynes-Roberts ◆ Manhattan Apartment, Library ◆ New York City, New York, USA ◆ 2011

164 Jimmy Jamieson and Susan Barrett ◆ St. Louis Guest House, Great Hall ◆ St. Louis, Missouri, USA ◆ 2020

Joe Columbo ◆ Visiona I, Bedroom ◆ Milan, Lombardy, Italy ◆ 1968

Redd Kaihoi • Upstate New York Home, Sitting Room • New York, USA • 2022

Maryam Mahdavi ◆ Paris Apartment, Tented Sitting Area ◆ Paris, France ◆ 2020

John Nash for the Prince of Wales ♦ Brighton Pavilion, Salon ♦ Brighton, East Sussex, England, UK ♦ 1823

Ludwig II of Bavaria ◆ Neuschwanstein Castle, Sitting Room ◆ Hohenschwangau, Bavaria, Germany, 1884

Daniel Garrett, James Paine, and Robert Adam • Alnwick Castle, Drawing Room • Alnwick, Northumberland, England, UK • 1760

House of Hackney ◆ Trematon Castle, Drawing Room ◆ Saltash, Cornwall, England, UK ◆ 2021

Elvis Presley • Graceland, Piano Room • Memphis, Tennessee, USA • 1965

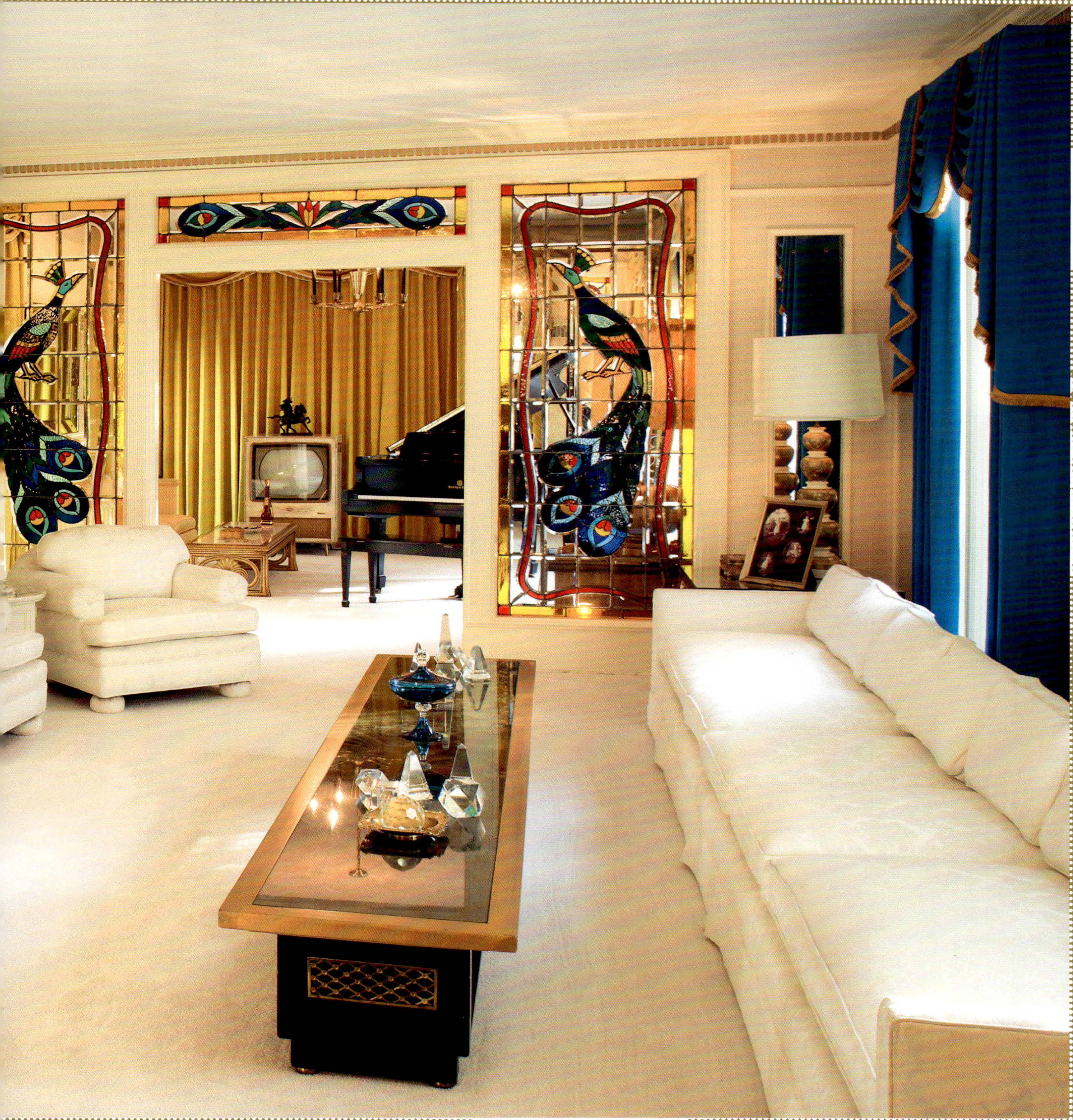

Greg Natale ◆ Barwon River House, Entry Foyer ◆ Melbourne, Victoria, Australia ◆ 2017

Jonathan Adler ◆ Jonathan Adler and Simon Doonan's Apartment, Living Room ◆ New York City, New York, USA ◆ 2018

Greg Natale • Horizon Apartment, Living Room • Sydney, New South Wales, Australia • 2019

Brock Forsblom ◆ West Village Apartment, Dining Area ◆ New York City, New York, USA ◆ 2017

Harry Heissmann • SoHo Holiday House, Bedroom • New York City, New York, USA • 2017

Smallwood Architects ◆ Georgian Shooting Lodge, Dining Hall ◆ Hampshire, England, UK ◆ 2011

Sam Cox (Mr. Doodle) ◆ Doodle House, Entrance Hall ◆ Tenterden, Kent, England, UK ◆ 2022

Viktor Udzenija ◆ London Pied-à-Terre, Living Room ◆ London, England, UK ◆ 2020

Ann Getty ◆ Getty Residence, Living Room ◆ San Francisco, California, USA ◆ 1987

Tony Duquette and Hutton Wilkinson ◆ Palazzo Brandolini, Coral Ballroom ◆ Venice, Veneto, Italy ◆ 1999

Richard Morris Hunt (architect) and Jules Allard (decorator) • Marble House, Gold Salon • Newport, Rhode Island, USA • 1892

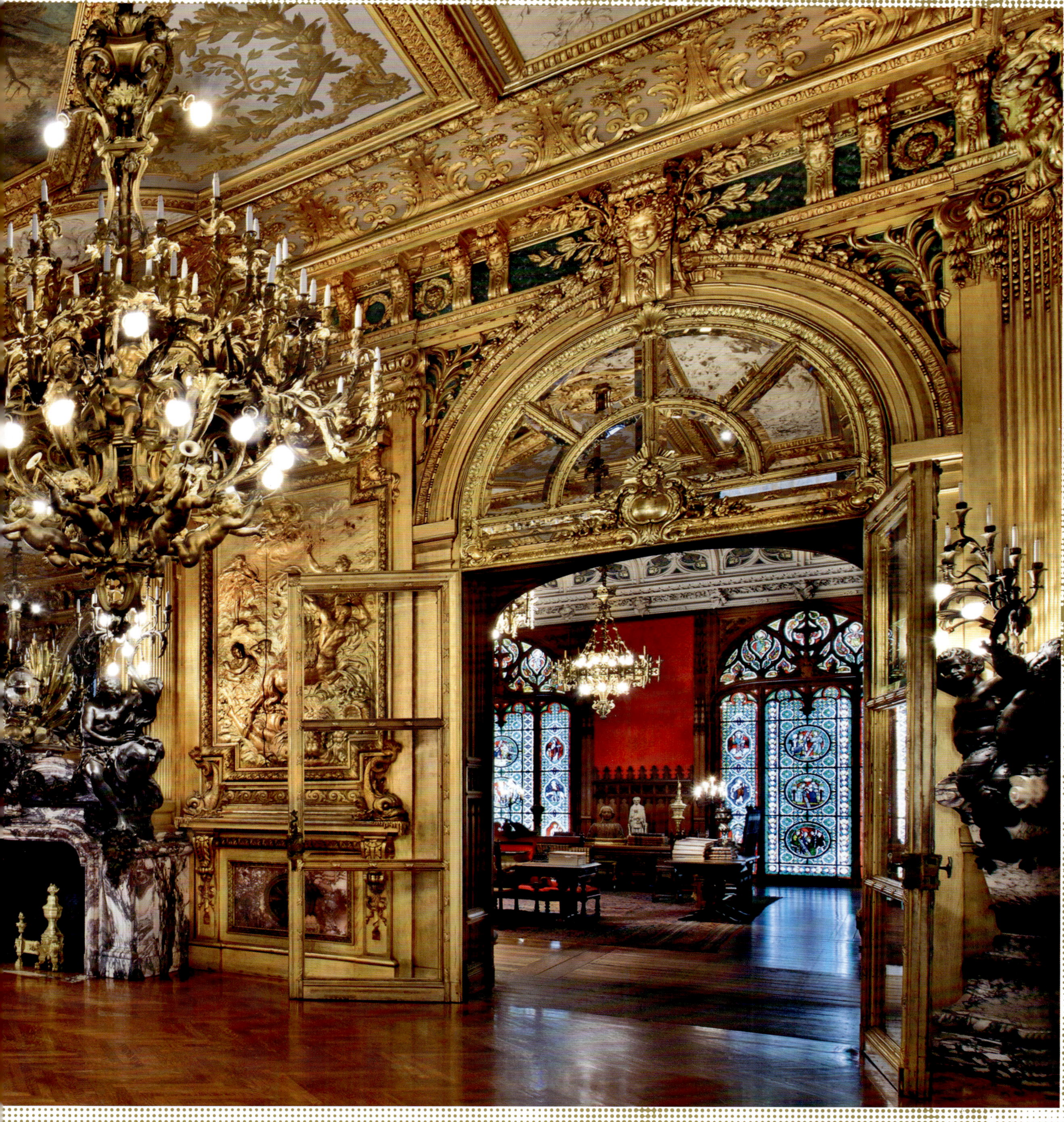

Renzo Mongiardino • Carraro Residence, Drawing Room • Rome, Lazio, Italy • 1975

Sir John Vanbrugh ◆ Blenheim Palace, Dining Room ◆ Woodstock, Oxfordshire, England, UK ◆ 1722

Renzo Mongiardino for Elsa Peretti ◆ La Torre, Living Room ◆ Porto Ercole, Tuscany, Italy ◆ 1989

Jacques Garcia • Château du Champ de Bataille, Gold Salon • Eure, Normandy, France • 1990

Tony Duquette and Hutton Wilkinson ◆ Palazzo Brandolini, Tiepolo Salon ◆ Venice, Veneto, Italy ◆ 1985

Louis Le Vaux • Palace of Versailles, Salon d'Abondance • Versailles, Île-de-France, France • 1680

Jacques Grange • Paris Apartment, Dining Room • Paris, France • 1980

Wharton Esherick • Wharton Esherick Studio • Township, Pennsylvania, USA • 1956

Gert Voorjans ◆ Voorjans Home and Studio, Living Room ◆ Antwerp, Belgium ◆ 2016

Roberto Polo ◆ Roberto Polo Residence, Library ◆ Toledo, Spain ◆ 2020

DON'T WEAR ONE RING, WEAR FIVE OR SIX. PEOPLE ASK HOW I CAN PLAY WITH ALL THOSE RINGS, AND I REPLY, VERY WELL, THANK YOU.

LIBERACE

Lluís Domènech i Montaner ◆ Casa Navàs, Upper Hall ◆ Reus, Catalonia, Spain ◆ 1908

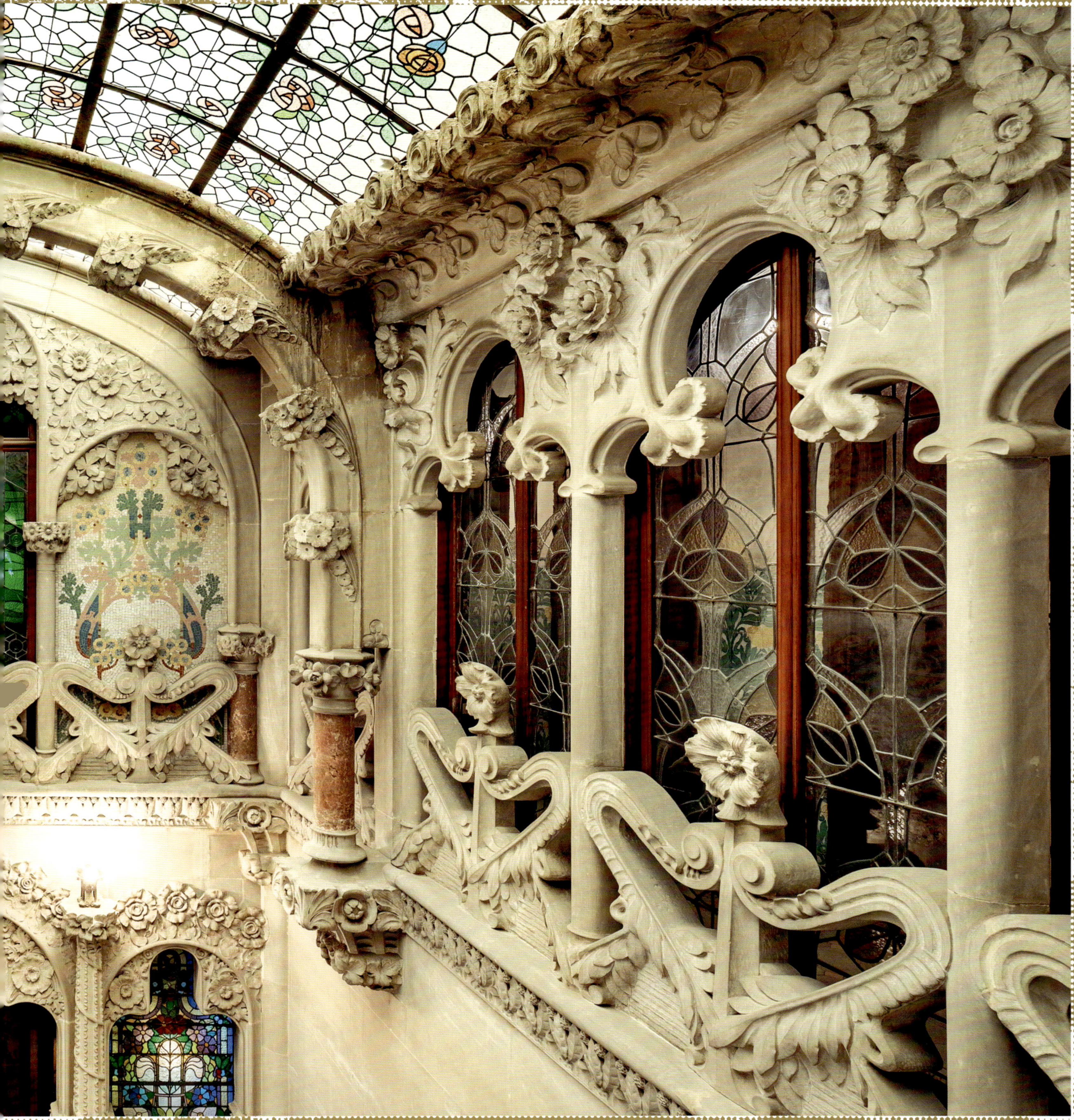

Francis II of Bourbon ◆ Royal Palace of Caserta, Bedroom of King Francis II of Bourbon ◆ Caserta, Campania, Italy ◆ 1840

Jonathan Adler ◆ Jonathan Adler and Simon Doonan's Apartment, Dining Room ◆ New York City, New York, USA ◆ 2018

Anthony Baratta ◆ Captiva Island Residence, Dining Room ◆ Captiva Island, Florida, USA ◆ 2008

Dorothy Draper • Greenbrier Hotel, Clock Lobby • White Sulphur Springs, West Virginia, USA • 1948

Marc-Antoine Wynant • Marcant Home, Lounge Area • Belgium • 2018

Jorge Pardo ◆ Jorge Pardo Residence, Living Room ◆ Brooklyn, New York, USA ◆ 2020

Frank di Biasi & Gene Meyer • Park Avenue Residence, Dining Room • New York City, New York, USA • 2017

Dani Dazey ◆ Trixie Motel, Yeehaw Cowgirl Suite ◆ Palm Springs, California, USA ◆ 2022

Ann Getty with Parish-Hadley • Pacific Heights Residence, Dining Room • San Francisco, California, USA • 1979

Hutton Wilkinson ◆ Caldwell Apartment, Living Room ◆ New York City, New York, USA ◆ 2014

Anne Pyne, McMillen Inc • Upper East Side Townhouse, Library • New York City, New York, USA • 2013

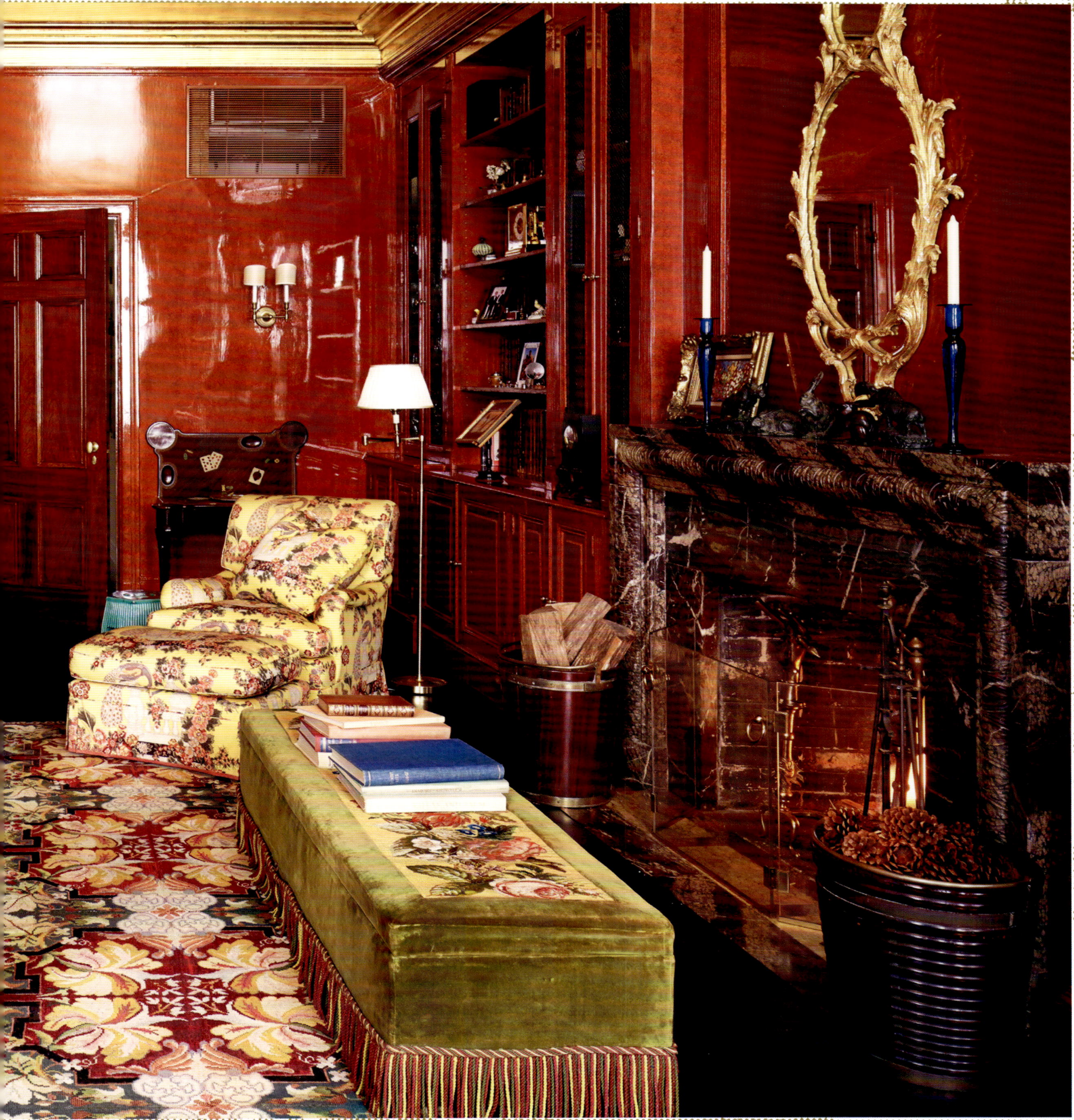

Count Otto Thott ♦ Gavnø Castle, Bedroom ♦ Gavnø, Zealand, Denmark ♦ 1758

Liza Bruce and Nicholas Alvis Vega ◆ Jaipur Jewel Apartment, Living Room ◆ Jaipur, Rajasthan, India ◆ 2010

William Georgis • Kips Bay Showhouse, Sitting Room • New York City, New York, USA • 2014

Dita Von Teese ◆ Von Teese Residence, Living Room ◆ Los Angeles, California, USA ◆ 2018

Tony Duquette and Hutton Wilkinson ◆ Duquette Ranch, 'Sortelegium', Tea House ◆ Malibu, California, USA ◆ 1995

Cindy Adams ◆ Park Avenue Apartment, Library ◆ New York City, New York, USA ◆ 2019

Thomas Britt • New York Apartment, Tent Room • New York City, New York, USA • 2007

Sigmund Freud ◆ Freud House, Study ◆ London, England, UK ◆ 1938

Demi Lovato • Los Angeles Farmhouse, 'Shroom Room' • Los Angeles, California, USA • 2022

Kravitz Design in collaboration with Disco Volante ♦ Williams Residence, Bedroom ♦ Beverly Hills, California, USA ♦ 2018

Kelly Wearstler • Bel Air Mansion, Entry Hall • Los Angeles, California, USA • 2012

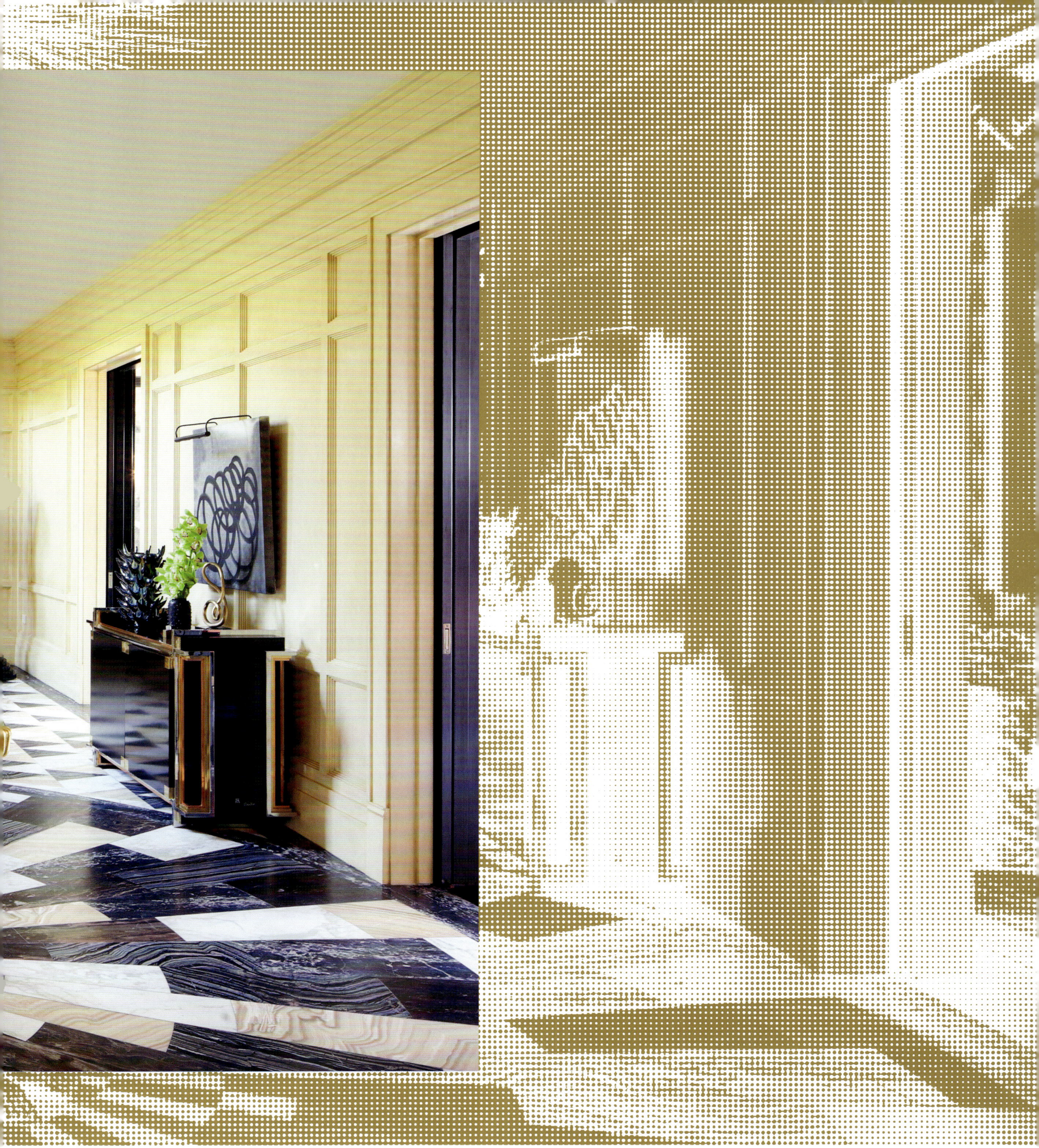

Miles Redd • New York Apartment, Hallway • New York City, New York, USA • 2007

Jimmy Jamieson and Susan Barrett ◆ St. Louis Guest House, Great Hall ◆ St. Louis, Missouri, USA ◆ 2020

Amaro Sánchez de Moya • Collector's House, Living Room • Seville, Andalusia, Spain • 2018

Juan Pablo Molyneux ◆ Pebble Beach Residence, Dining Room ◆ Pebble Beach, California, USA ◆ 2013

Maharajah of Jaipur ◆ Jaipur City Palace, Blue Hall ◆ Jaipur, Rajasthan, India ◆ 1727

Tory Burch ◆ Manhattan Residence, Sitting Room ◆ New York City, New York, USA ◆ 2010

King Louis XIV • Château de Chambord, Queen's Bedroom • Chambord, Centre-Val de Loire, France • 1680

Hutton Wilkinson and Tony Duquette ◆ Manhattan Penthouse, Dining Room ◆ New York City, New York, USA ◆ 2019

Daniel Garrett, James Paine and Robert Adam ◆ Alnwick Castle, Drawing Room ◆ Alnwick, Northumberland, England, UK ◆ 1760

Edward James • Monkton House, Living Room • Chilgrove, West Sussex, England, UK • 1930

I DON'T CARE WHAT YOU THINK ABOUT ME. I DON'T THINK ABOUT YOU AT ALL.

GABRIELLE CHANEL

236 Miles Redd and David Kaihoi ◆ Family Lodge, Main Bedroom ◆ Adirondack Park, New York, USA ◆ 2019

237

Mario Buatta • Manhattan Apartment, Library • New York City, New York, USA • 1997

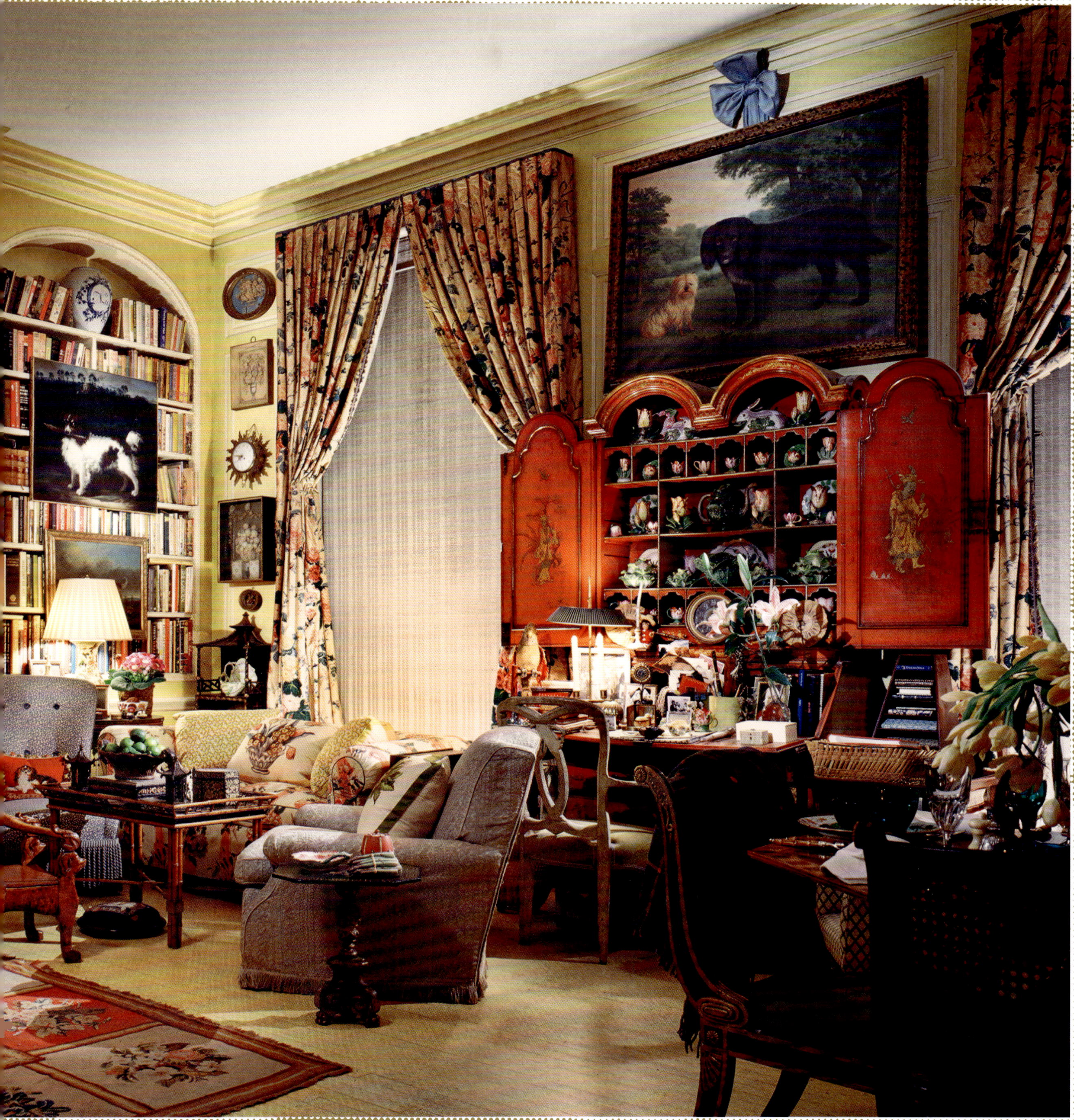

240 • Jonathan Adler • Jonathan Adler and Simon Doonan's Apartment, Dressing Room • New York City, New York, USA • 2018

Redd Kaihoi ◆ Upstate New York Home, Living Room ◆ New York, USA ◆ 2022

Georg Wenzeslaus von Knobelsdorff for King Frederick the Great ◆ Schloss Sanssouci, Voltaire Room ◆ Potsdam, Germany ◆ 1747

Jonathan Adler ◆ Shelter Island House, Living Room ◆ Shelter Island, New York, USA ◆ 2011

Henri Samuel for Louise de Vilmorin • Château Verrières-le-Buisson, Salon Bleu • Verrières-le-Buisson, Île-de-France, France • 1959

Francesca DiMattio • Manhattan Townhouse, Dining Room • New York City, New York, USA • 2022

Greg Natale • Melbourne House, Living Room • Melbourne, Victoria, Australia • 2022

Richard Mishaan • New York Apartment, Living Room • New York City, New York, USA • 2014

Julia Morgan for William Randolph Hearst • Hearst Castle, Main Library • San Simeon, California, USA • 1947

Amaro Sánchez de Moya ◆ Collector's House, Living Room ◆ Seville, Andalusia, Spain ◆ 2018

Ken Fulk ◆ Cypress Grove, Dining Room ◆ San Francisco, California, USA ◆ 2015

251

Mario Buatta • Mehle Residence, Living Room • New York City, New York, USA • 2017

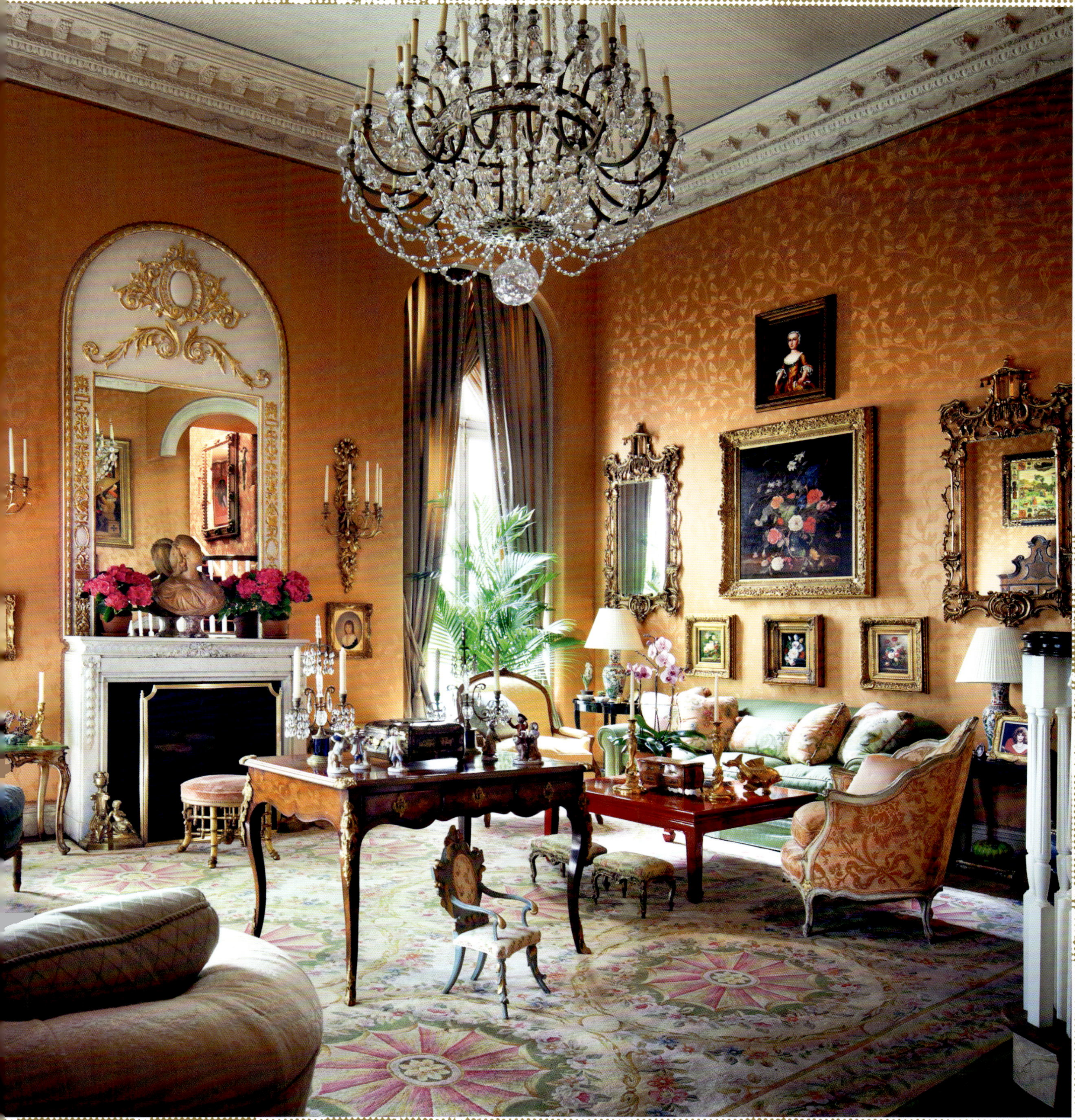

Deborah Turbeville • Casa No Name, Sitting Room • San Miguel de Allende, Guanajuato, Mexico • 1985

Oscar de la Renta • de la Renta Apartment, Living Room • New York City, New York, USA • 1969

Geoffrey Bennison • Paris Apartment, Salon • Paris, France • 1985

Jacques Grange for Pierre Bergé ◆ La Datcha, Living Room ◆ Benerville-sur-Mer, Normandy, France ◆ 1989

Gwynn Griffith • San Antonio Factory Residence, Sitting Room • San Antonio, Texas, USA • 2011

Greg Natale ♦ Barwon River House, Bar ♦ Melbourne, Victoria, Australia ♦ 2017

Elsie de Wolfe ◆ Villa Trianon, Salon ◆ Versailles, Île-de-France, France ◆ 1906

Billy Haines ♦ Sunnylands, Atrium and Living Room ♦ Palm Springs, California, USA ♦ 1966

Anthony Baratta • Southern California Château, Living Room • Los Angeles, California, USA • 2014

Stacey Bendet and Louise Kugelberg ◆ Manhattan Apartment, Living Room ◆ New York City, New York, USA ◆ 2022

Amaro Sánchez de Moya ♦ Collector's House, Sitting Room ♦ Seville, Andalusia, Spain ♦ 2018

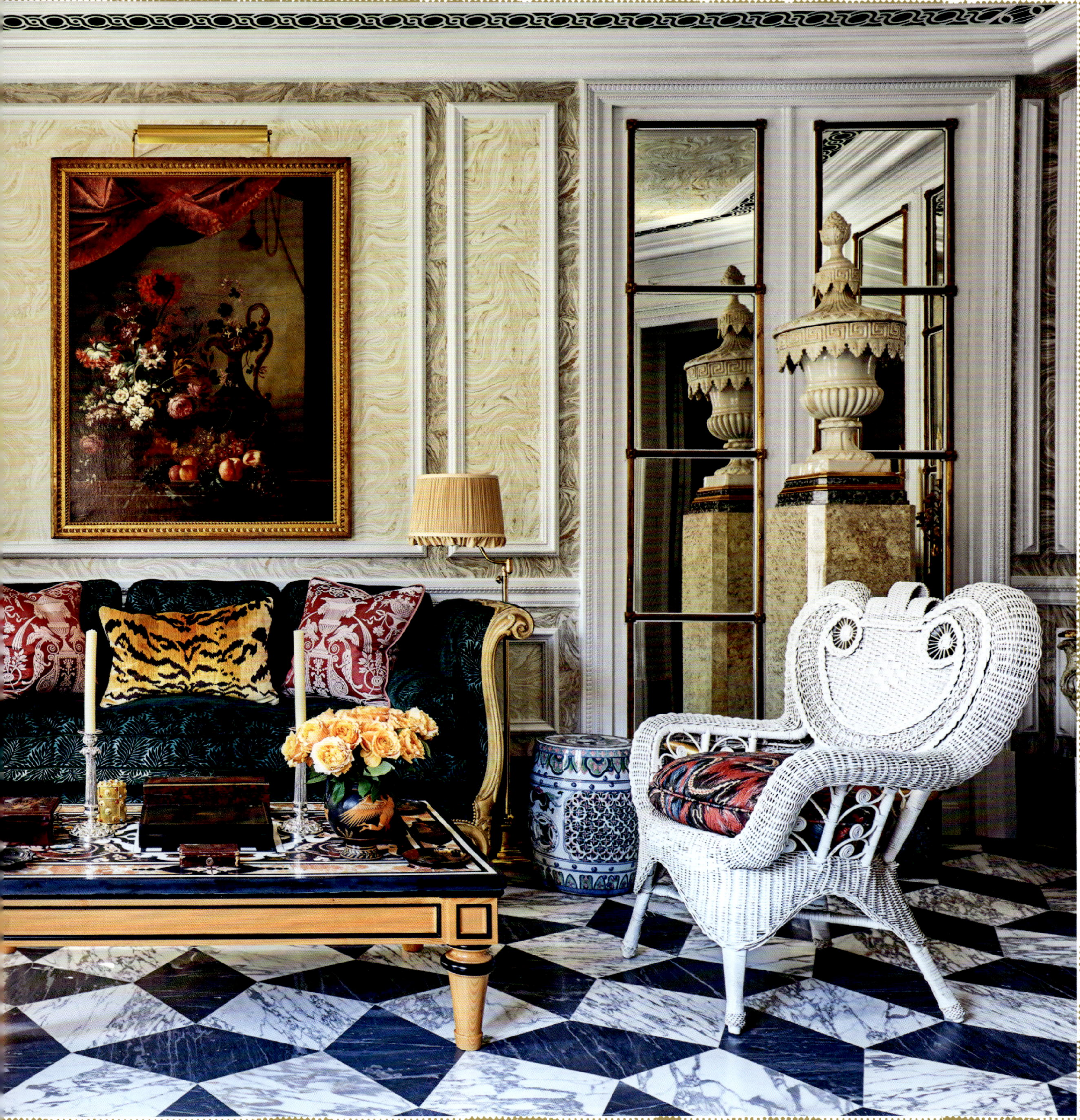

Job Smeets ♦ Studio Job Headquarters, Salon ♦ Antwerp, Belgium ♦ 2018

Ann Getty ◆ Getty Residence, Drawing Room ◆ San Francisco, California, USA ◆ 1987

Cindy Adams ◆ Cindy Adams' Apartment, Studio ◆ New York City, New York, USA ◆ 1997

Miles Redd and David Kaihoi ◆ Upstate New York Home, Living Room ◆ New York, USA ◆ 2022

Alidad ◆ Kuwait Villa, Library ◆ Kuwait City, Kuwait ◆ 2013

Alidad • London Residence, Dining Room • London, England, UK • 2013

William George Spencer Cavendish, Sixth Duke of Devonshire ◆ Chatsworth House, Library ◆ Derbyshire, England, UK ◆ 1832

Ann Getty ◆ Getty Residence, Bedroom ◆ San Francisco, California, USA ◆ 1987

Ruthie Sommers ◆ Chicago Mansion, Sitting Room ◆ Chicago, Illinois, USA ◆ 2021

Greg Natale • Barwon River House, Bar • Melbourne, Victoria, Australia • 2017

Steven Gambrel • Upper East Side Apartment, Library • New York City, New York, USA • 2013

Richard Morris Hunt (architect) and Jules Allard (decorator) ◆ Marble House, Dining Room ◆ Newport, Rhode Island, USA ◆ 1892

I THOUGHT VAN DER ROHE WAS AN IDIOT. LESS IS MORE. HOW STUPID CAN YOU BE. LESS IS NOT MORE. LESS IS NOTHING.

MORRIS LAPIDUS

TIMELINE

SEVENTEENTH CENTURY

1653
Wilton House, Double Cube Room
Inigo Jones for the Earl of Pembroke
Wilton, Wiltshire, England, UK
Page 123

1666
Topkapi Palace, Imperial Hall
Sultan Osman III
Istanbul, Turkey
Page 94

1680
Château de Chambord, Queen's Bedroom
King Louis XIV
Chambord, Centre-Val de Loire, France
Page 230

Château de Chambord, Ceremonial Bedroom of Louis XIV
King Louis XIV
Chambord, Centre-Val de Loire, France
Page 68

Palace of Versailles, Salon d'Abondance
Louis Le Vaux
Versailles, Île-de-France, France
Page 191

1686
Palace of Versailles, War Room
Hardouin-Mansart for Louis XIV
Versailles, Île-de-France, France
Page 28

1687
Trianon Palace, Salon des Glaces
Jules Hardouin-Mansart
Versailles, Île-de-France, France
Page 88

EIGHTEENTH CENTURY

1722
Blenheim Palace, Dining Room
Sir John Vanbrugh
Woodstock, Oxfordshire, England, UK
Page 187

1726
Old Royal Naval College, Painted Hall
Sir James Thornhill
London, England, UK
Page 156

1727
Jaipur City Palace, Chandra Mahal, Shobha Niwas (Hall of Beauty)
Maharaja Sawai Jai Singh II
Jaipur, Rajasthan, India
Page 36

Jaipur City Palace, Blue Hall
Maharajah of Jaipur
Jaipur, Rajasthan, India
Page 228

1737
Château de Chantilly, Grand Singerie
Christophe Huet
Chantilly, Hauts-de-France, France
Page 34

1747
Schloss Sanssouci, Voltaire Room
Georg Wenzeslaus von Knobelsdorff for King Frederick the Great
Potsdam, Brandenburg, Germany
Page 242

1758
Gavnø Castle, Bedroom
Count Otto Thott
Gavnø, Zealand, Denmark
Page 212

1760
Alnwick Castle, Dining Room
Daniel Garrett, James Paine and Robert Adam
Alnwick, Northumberland, England, UK
Page 232

Alnwick Castle, Drawing Room
Daniel Garrett, James Paine and Robert Adam
Alnwick, Northumberland, England, UK
Page 170

1765
Castle Schönbrunn, Napoleon Room
Nikolaus Pacassi for Maria Theresa, Ruler of the Habsburg Empire
Vienna, Austria
Page 30

NINETEENTH CENTURY

1820
Buckingham Palace, White Drawing Room
John Nash
London, England, UK
Page 18

1823
Brighton Pavilion, Salon
John Nash (architect), Frederick Crace and Robert Jones (interiors) for the Prince of Wales, later King George IV
Brighton, East Sussex, England, UK
Page 168

1832
Chatsworth House, Library
William George Spencer Cavendish, 6th Duke of Devonshire
Derbyshire, England, UK
Page 272

1840
Royal Palace of Caserta, Bedroom of King Francis II of Bourbon
Francis II of Bourbon
Caserta, Campania, Italy
Page 200

1854
Pena Palace, Arabic Room
Ferdinand II
Sintra, Portugal
Page 121

1864
Castillo de Chapultepec, Emperor's Music Room
José de la Cruz Porfirio Díaz Mori
Mexico City, Mexico
Page 136

1869
London Northwestern Railway, Queen Victoria's Royal Saloon
Richard Bore for Queen Victoria
London, England, UK
Page 100

1883
Waddesdon Manor, Tower Drawing Room
Baron Ferdinand de Rothschild
Buckinghamshire, England, UK
Page 138

1884
Neuschwanstein Castle, Sitting Room
Ludwig II of Bavaria
Hohenschwangau, Bavaria, Germany
Page 169

Neuschwanstein Castle, Bedroom
Ludwig II of Bavaria
Hohenschwangau, Bavaria, Germany
Page 75

1885
Casa Vicens, Smoking Room
Antoni Gaudí
Barcelona, Catalonia, Spain
Page 162

1892
Marble House, Dining Room
Richard Morris Hunt (architect) and Jules Allard (decorator)
Newport, Rhode Island, USA
Page 277

Marble House, Gold Salon
Richard Morris Hunt (architect) and Jules Allard (decorator)
Newport, Rhode Island, USA
Page 184

1897
Drottningholm Palace, Porcelain Room
Nicodemus Tessin the Elder and Nicodemus Tessin the Younger for Queen Dowager Regent Hedwig Eleonora
Stockholm, Sweden
Page 97

TWENTIETH CENTURY

1906
Villa Trianon, Salon
Elsie de Wolfe
Versailles, Île-de-France, France
Page 260

1908
Casa Navàs, Vestibule
Lluís Domènech i Montaner
Reus, Catalonia, Spain
Page 96

Casa Navàs, Upper Hall
Lluís Domènech i Montaner
Reus, Catalonia, Spain
Page 198

1913
Port Lympne Mansion, Tent Room
Rex Whistler for Sir Philip Sassoon
Port Lympne, Kent, England, UK
Page 124

1915
Planting Fields Foundation, Tea House
Elsie de Wolfe
Oyster Bay, New York, USA
Page 59

1922
Villa Vizcaya, Bedroom
James Deering and Paul Chalfin
Miami, Florida, USA
Page 74

1930
Monkton House, Living Room
Edward James
Chilgrove, West Sussex, England, UK
Page 233

1938
Freud House, Study
Sigmund Freud
London, England, UK
Page 219

1947
Hearst Castle, Main Library
Julia Morgan for William Randolph Hearst
San Simeon, California, USA
Page 248

1948
Greenbrier Hotel, Lobby
Dorothy Draper
White Sulphur Springs,
West Virginia, USA
Page 144

Greenbriar Hotel, Clock Lobby
Dorothy Draper
White Sulphur Springs,
West Virginia, USA
Page 203

Greenbriar Hotel, Presidential Suite
Dorothy Draper
White Sulphur Springs,
West Virginia, USA
Page 51

Greenbriar Hotel, Presidential Suite
Dorothy Draper
White Sulphur Springs,
West Virginia, USA
Page 58

1955
Park Avenue Apartment, Living Room
Billy Baldwin for Diana Vreeland
New York City, New York, USA
Page 41

Dawnridge, Drawing Room
Tony Duquette & Hutton Wilkinson
Beverly Hills, California, USA
Page 76

Dawnridge, Garden Room
Tony Duquette & Hutton Wilkinson
Beverly Hills, California, USA
Page 40

1956
Wharton Esherick Studio
Wharton Esherick
Township, Pennsylvania, USA
Page 193

1959
Château Verrières-le-Buisson,
Salon Bleu
Henri Samuel for Louise de Vilmorin
Verrières-le-Buisson, Île-de-France,
France
Page 244

1963
Château de Groussay, Tartar Tent
Emilio Terry and Carlos de Beistegui
Montfort-l'Amaury, Île-de-France,
France
Page 149

1965
Graceland, Bedroom
Elvis Presley
Memphis, Tennessee, USA
Page 155

1966
Sunnylands, Atrium and Living Room
Billy Haines
Palm Springs, California, USA
Page 261

1968
Visiona I, Bedroom
Joe Columbo
Milan, Lombardy, Italy
Page 165

1969
de la Renta Apartment, Living Room
Oscar de la Renta
New York City, New York, USA
Page 255

1970
Roman Penthouse, Turkish
Tent Alcove
Valentino
Rome, Lazio, Italy
Page 115

1972
Vistorta, Conservatory
Countess Cristiana Brandolini D'Adda
Pordenone, Friuli-Venezia Giulia, Italy
Page 105

1972
Graceland, TV Room
Elvis Presley
Memphis, Tennessee, USA
Page 61

The Liberace Mansion, Living Room
Liberace
Las Vegas, Nevada, USA
Page 127

1974
Graceland, Jungle Room
Elvis Presley
Memphis, Tennessee, USA
Page 81

Graceland, Piano Room
Elvis Presley
Memphis, Tennessee, USA
Page 172

Graceland, Music Room
Elvis Presley
Memphis, Tennessee, USA
Page 62

1975
Carraro Residence, Drawing Room
Renzo Mongiardino
Rome, Lazio, Italy
Page 186

1977
Upper East Side Apartment, Library
Denning & Fourcade
New York City, New York, USA
Page 110

1978
Apfel Residence, Sitting Room
Iris Apfel
New York City, New York, USA
Page 78

1979
Pacific Heights Residence,
Dining Room
Ann Getty with Parish-Hadley
San Francisco, California, USA
Page 208

Pacific Heights Residence,
Sitting Room
Ann Getty with Parish-Hadley
San Francisco, California, USA
Page 20

1980
Palais Bulle, Living Room
Antti Lovag
Théoule sur Mer, Provence-
Alpes-Côte d'Azur, France
Page 108

Paris Apartment, Dining Room
Jacques Grange
Paris, France
Page 192

1985
Casa No Name, Sitting Room
Deborah Turbeville
San Miguel de Allende, Guanajuato,
Mexico
Page 254

Paris Apartment, Salon
Geoffrey Bennison
Paris, France
Page 256

Paris Apartment, Dining Room
Rudolf Nureyev
Paris, France
Page 24

Paris Apartment, Living Room
Rudolf Nureyev
Paris, France
Page 84

Palazzo Brandolini, Tiepolo Salon
Tony Duquette & Hutton Wilkinson
Venice, Veneto, Italy
Page 190

1987
Getty Residence, Sitting Room
Ann Getty
San Francisco, California, USA
Page 44

London House, Living Room
Anthony Collett
London, England, UK
Page 26

Fifth Avenue Apartment, Living Room
Henri Samuel for Susan Gutfreund
New York City, New York, USA
Page 38

Getty Residence, Bedroom
Ann Getty
San Francisco, California, USA
Page 273

Getty Residence, Living Room
Ann Getty
San Francisco, California, USA
Page 182

Getty Residence, Drawing Room
Ann Getty
San Francisco, California, USA
Page 267

Getty Residence, Dining Room
Ann Getty
San Francisco, California, USA
Page 104

1989
La Datcha, Living Room
Jacques Grange for Pierre Bergé
Benerville-sur-Mer, Normandy, France
Page 257

Paris House, Salon
Valerian Rybar and Jean-François Daigre
Paris, France
Page 33

La Torre, Living Room
Renzo Mongiardino for Elsa Peretti
Porto Ercole
Tuscany, Italy
Page 188

1990

Casa Casuarina, Bedroom
Gianni Versace
Miami, Florida, USA
Page 31

Château du Champ de Bataille, Apollo Salon
Jacques Garcia
Eure, Normandy, France
Page 72

Château du Champ de Bataille, Cabinet of Curiosities
Jacques Garcia
Eure, Normandy, France
Page 21

Château du Champ de Bataille, Gold Salon
Jacques Garcia
Eure, Normandy, France
Page 189

Château du Champ de Bataille, Salon Asiatique
Jacques Garcia
Eure, Normandy, France
Page 140

Casa Casuarina, Bedroom
Gianni Versace
Miami, Florida, USA
Page 146

1994

Versace Apartment, Living Room
Donatella Versace
Milan, Lombardy, Italy
Page 85

1995

New York Apartment, Sitting Room
Denning & Fourcade
New York City, New York, USA
Page 32

Duquette Ranch, 'Sortelegium', Tea House
Tony Duquette & Hutton Wilkinson
Malibu, California, USA
Page 216

1997

Miami House, Living Room
Sylvester Stallone
Miami, Florida, USA
Page 107

Manhattan Apartment, Library
Mario Buatta
New York City, New York, USA
Page 238
1997

Manhattan Apartment, Sitting Room
Mario Buatta
New York City, New York, USA
Page 118

Cindy Adams' Apartment, Studio
Cindy Adams
New York City, New York, USA
Page 268

1999

Palazzo Brandolini, Coral Ballroom
Tony Duquette & Hutton Wilkinson
Venice, Veneto, Italy
Page 183

TWENTY-FIRST CENTURY

2006

Parisian Pied-à-Terre, Drawing Room
Alidad
Paris, France
Page 122

Reyes Residence, Kitchen and Sitting Area
Jorge Pardo
Naguabo Playa, Puerto Rico
Page 52

2007

Patricia Altschul Residence, Dining Room
Mario Buatta
New York City, New York, USA
Page 80

New York Apartment, Hallway
Miles Redd
New York City, New York, USA
Page 224

South Wraxall Manor, Drawing Room
Robert Kime
South Wraxall, Wiltshire, England, UK
Page 82

New York Apartment, Tent Room
Thomas Britt
New York City, New York, USA
Page 218

2008

London Townhouse
Alidad
London, England, UK
Page 137

Captiva Island Residence, Dining Room
Anthony Baratta
Captiva Island, Florida, USA
Page 202

Paris Apartment, Living Room
Rose Anne de Pampelonne
Paris, France
Page 53

Baratta Apartment, Living Room
Anthony Baratta
Miami, Florida, USA
Page 48

2009

Les Prés d'Eugénie, Empress Aisle Salon
Guérard Family
Eugénie-les-Bains, Nouvelle-Aquitaine, France
Page 25

2010

Jaipur Jewel Apartment, Living Room
Liza Bruce & Nicholas Alvis Vega
Jaipur, Rajasthan, India
Page 213

Manhattan Residence, Sitting Room
Tory Burch
New York City, New York, USA
Page 229

2011

Manhattan Apartment, Library
Haynes-Roberts
New York City, New York, USA
Page 163

Shelter Island House, Living Room
Jonathan Adler
Shelter Island, New York, USA
Page 243

Bellagio Residence, Dressing Room
Kelly Wearstler
Los Angeles, California, USA
Page 120

Aileen Mehle Residence, Dining Room
Mario Buatta
New York City, New York, USA
Page 42

Georgian Shooting Lodge, Dining Hall
Smallwood Architects
Hampshire, England, UK
Page 179

Lyford Cay Club House, Main Drawing Room
Tom Scheerer
Nassau, New Providence, Bahamas
Page 19

San Antonio Factory Residence, Sitting Room
Gwynn Griffith
San Antonio, Texas, USA
Page 258

New York City Residence, Home Office
Robert Couturier
New York City, New York, USA
Page 23

2012

Kuwait Residence, Library
Alidad
Kuwait City, Kuwait
Page 160

Mayfair Pied-à-Terre, Sitting Room
Alidad
London, England, UK
Page 147

Kuwait Residence, Sitting Room
Alidad
Kuwait City, Kuwait
Page 69

Bel Air Mansion, Living Room
Kelly Wearstler
Los Angeles, California, USA
Page 150

Bel Air Mansion, Entry Hall
Kelly Wearstler
Los Angeles, California, USA
Page 222

Summer House, Living Room, and Bar
Bradford Shellhammer
Orange County, New York, USA
Page 66

2013

London Residence, Dining Room
Alidad
London, England, UK
Page 271

Kuwait Villa
Alidad
Kuwait City, Kuwait
Page 270

Pebble Beach Residence, Dining Room
Juan Pablo Molyneux
Pebble Beach, California, USA
Page 227

Brooklyn Townhouse, Living Room
Nick Olsen
Brooklyn, New York, USA
Page 27

Upper East Side Apartment, Library
Steven Gambrel
New York City, New York, USA
Page 276

Upper East Side Townhouse, Library
Anne Pyne, McMillen Inc.
New York City, New York, USA
Page 210

Pied-à-Terre, Living Room
Thomas Britt
San Francisco, California, USA
Page 141

2014

Martyn Thompson, Studio
Martyn Thompson
New York City, New York, USA
Page 102

East Village Loft, Living Room
Roger de Cabrol
New York City, New York, USA
Page 67

Southern California Château,
Living Room
Anthony Baratta
Los Angeles, California, USA
Page 262

Kips Bay Showhouse, Sitting Room
William Georgis
New York City, New York, USA
Page 214

New York Apartment, Living Room
Richard Mishaan
New York City, New York, USA
Page 247

Caldwell Apartment, Living Room
Hutton Wilkinson
New York City, New York, USA
Page 209

2015

Pink House, Living Room
Anthony Baratta
New York City, New York, USA
Page 109

Queens Apartment,
Sleeping Area
Brett Leemkuil
Queens, New York, USA
Page 70

Cypress Grove, Dining Room
Ken Fulk
San Francisco, California, USA
Page 250

Milan Residence, Living Room
Lapo Elkann
Milan, Lombardy, Italy
Page 90

Pedro Espírito Santo Residence,
Salon
Pedro Espírito Santo
Lisbon, Portugal
Page 125

São Paulo Estate, Living Room
Sig Bergamin
São Paulo, Brazil
116

Kagan Apartment,
Living Room
Vladimir Kagan
New York City, New York, USA
Page 49

Malibu Home, Bedroom
Hutton Wilkinson
Los Angeles, California, USA
Page 139

San Francisco House, Dining Room
Sheldon Harte
San Francisco, California, USA
Page 148

2016

Voorjans Home and Studio,
Living Room
Gert Voorjans
Antwerp, Belgium
Page 194

Hong Kong Apartment, Dining Room
Mattia Bonetti
Hong Kong, China
Page 92

Private Residence, Living Room
Alisha Gwen
Gibsonia, Pennsylvania, USA
Page 65

Houston Home, Living Room
Celerie Kemble and Lindsey Herod
Houston, Texas, USA
Page 56

2017

The Albany, Living Room
Ashley Hicks
London, England, UK
Page 47

West Village Apartment, Dining Area
Brock Forsblom
New York City, New York, USA
Page 177

Park Avenue Residence, Dining Room
Frank di Biasi & Gene Meyer
New York City, New York, USA
Page 206

Barwon River House, Entry Foyer
Greg Natale
Melbourne, Victoria, Australia
174

Barwon River House, Bar
Greg Natale
Melbourne, Victoria, Australia
Page 259

Barwon River House, Bar
Greg Natale
Melbourne, Victoria, Australia
Page 275

SoHo Holiday House, Bedroom
Harry Heissmann
New York City, New York, USA
Page 178

Brooklyn Apartment, Sitting Room
James Aguiar
Brooklyn, New York, USA
Page 77

Farmhouse, Bedroom
Oberto Gili
Turin, Piedmont, Italy
Page 73

Paris Apartment, Dining Room
Rouge Absolu
Paris, France
Page 111

Barwon River House, Living Room
Greg Natale
Melbourne, Victoria, Australia
Page 98

Mehle Residence, Living Room
Mario Buatta
New York City, New York, USA
Page 252

Nisbet Residence, Living Room
Amanda Nisbet Design
New York City, New York, USA
Page 64

2018

Collector's House, Living Room
Amaro Sánchez de Moya
Seville, Andalusia, Spain
Page 226

Von Teese Residence, Living Room
Dita Von Teese
Los Angeles, California, USA
Page 215

LA Home, Kitchen and DIning Room
Kelly Wearstler
Los Angeles, California, USA
Page 134

Williams Residence, Bedroom
Kravitz Design in collaboration
with Disco Volante
Beverly Hills, California, USA
Page 221

Kips Bay Showhouse, Staircase
Sasha Bikoff
New York City, New York, USA
Page 63

Studio Job Headquarters, Salon
Job Smeets
Antwerp, Belgium
Page 266

Studio Job Headquarters,
Bedroom and Ensuite
Job Smeets
Antwerp, Belgium
Page 60

Jonathan Adler and Simon Doonan's
Apartment, Dining Room
Jonathan Adler
New York City, New York, USA
Page 201

Jonathan Adler and Simon Doonan's
Apartment, Living Room
Jonathan Adler
New York City, New York, USA
Page 175

Jonathan Adler and Simon Doonan's
Apartment, Bedroom
Jonathan Adler
New York City, New York, USA
Page 129

Jonathan Adler and Simon Doonan's
Apartment, Dressing Room
Jonathan Adler
New York City, New York, USA
Page 240

Collector's House, Living Room
Amaro Sánchez de Moya
Seville, Andalusia, Spain
Page 249

Collector's House, Sitting Room
Amaro Sánchez de Moya
Seville, Andalusia, Spain
Page 264

Von Teese Residence, Dining Room
Dita Von Teese
Los Angeles, California, USA
Page 95

Asolo Residence, Living and
Dining Area
Michela Goldschmied
Asolo, Veneto, Italy
Page 16

Eva Cavalli Home, Living Room
Eva Cavalli
Florence, Tuscany, Italy
Page 132

Marcant Home, Lounge Area
Marc-Antoine Wynant
Belgium
Page 204

Eva Cavalli Home, Living Room
Eva Cavalli
Florence, Tuscany, Italy
Page 22

2019

Woody House, Sitting Room
Peter Marino
Long Island, New York, USA
Page 128

Paris Apartment, Living Room
Alberto Pinto
Paris, France
Page 153

Park Avenue Apartment, Library
Cindy Adams
New York City, New York, USA
Page 217

Timeline

Manhattan Penthouse, Dining Room
Hutton Wilkinson and Tony Duquette
New York City, New York, USA
Page 231

Hacienda Buena Fe, Bedroom
Michelle Nussbaumer
San Miguel de Allende, Guanajuato, Mexico
Page 154

Family Lodge, Main Bedroom
Miles Redd and David Kaihoi
Adirondack Park, New York, USA
Page 236

Woody House, Living Room
Peter Marino
Long Island, New York, USA
Page 126

Horizon Apartment, Living Room
Greg Natale
Sydney, New South Wales, Australia
Page 176

Kips Bay Showhouse, Sitting Room
Young Huh Interior Design
New York City, New York, USA
Page 135

2020

De Gournay Showroom,
Private Apartment, Salon
India Mahdavi
Paris, France
Page 106

Jorge Pardo Residence, Living Room
Jorge Pardo
Brooklyn, New York, USA
Page 205

Joseph Holtzman Installation
Joseph Holzman
New York City, New York, USA
Page 50

Paris Apartment, Sitting Area
Maryam Mahdavi
Paris, France
Page 152

Paris Apartment, Tented Sitting Area
Maryam Mahdavi
Paris, France
Page 167

Nussbaumer Residence, Living Room
Michelle Nussbaumer
Dallas, Texas, USA
Page 143

St. Louis Guest House, Great Hall
Jimmy Jamieson and Susan Barrett
St. Louis, Missouri, USA
Page 164

Wilshire Corridor Penthouse,
Sitting Area
Tony Duquette & Hutton Wilkinson
Los Angeles, California, USA
Page 151

London Pied-à-Terre, Living Room
Viktor Udzenija
London, England, UK
Page 181

Roberto Polo Residence, Library
Roberto Polo
Toledo, Spain
Page 195

St. Louis Guest House, Drawing Room
Jimmy Jamieson and Susan Barrett
St. Louis, Missouri, USA
Page 142

St. Louis Guest House, Great Hall
Jimmy Jamieson and Susan Barrett
St. Louis, Missouri, USA
Page 225

2021

Toorak Penthouse, Dining Room
Greg Natale
Melbourne, Victoria, Australia
Page 113

Grisanti Residence, Living Room
Grisanti & Cussen
Santiago, Chile
Page 91

Trematon Castle, Hollyhocks Bedroom
House of Hackney
Saltash, Cornwall, England, UK
Page 114

Trematon Castle, Drawing Room
House of Hackney
Saltash, Cornwall, England, UK
Page 171

Trematon Castle, Flora Delanica Bedroom
House of Hackney
Saltash, Cornwall, England, UK
Page 79

Chicago Mansion, Sitting Room
Ruthie Sommers
Chicago, Illinois, USA
Page 274

2022

Trixie Motel, Yeehaw Cowgirl Suite
Dani Dazey
Palm Springs, California, USA
Page 207

Los Angeles Farmhouse,
'Shroom Room'
Demi Lovato
Los Angeles, California, USA
Page 220

Manhattan Townhouse, Dining Room
Francesca DiMattio
New York City, New York, USA
Page 245

Manhattan Townhouse, Living Room
Francesco DiMattio
New York City, New York, USA
Page 35

Melbourne House, Living Room
Greg Natale
Melbourne, Victoria, Australia
Page 246

Villa Palladio, Bar Palladio
Marie-Anne Oudejans
Jaipur, Rajasthan, India
Page 99

Upstate New York Home, Living Room
Miles Redd and David Kaihoi
New York, USA
Page 269

Upstate New York Home,
Sitting Room
Redd Kaihoi
New York, USA
Page 166

Upstate New York Home, Living Room
Redd Kaihoi
New York, USA
Page 241

Doodle House, Entrance Hall
Sam Cox (Mr. Doodle)
Tenterden, Kent, England, UK
Page 180

Manhattan Apartment, Living Room
Stacey Bendet and Louise Kugelberg
New York City, New York, USA
Page 263

Southern California Home,
Main Bedroom
Justina Blakeney
California, USA
Page 46

Laurent di Benedetto Residence,
Living Room
Teo Leo Galerie
Paris, France
Page 93

Trixie Motel, Pink Flamingo Suite
Dani Dazey
Palm Springs, California, USA
Page 112

Trixie Motel, Atomic Bombshell Room
Dani Dazey
Palm Springs, California, USA
Page 101

INDEX

A

Adam, Robert 170, 232
Adams, Cindy
   Cindy Adams' Apartment 268
   Park Avenue Apartment 217
Adler, Jonathan 11, 13
   Jonathan Adler and Simon Doonan's Apartment 129, 175, 201, 240
   Shelter Island House 243
Aguiar, James 77
Aileen Mehle Residence, New York City 42–3
The Albany, London 47
Alidad
   Kuwait Residence 69, 160–1
   Kuwait Villa 270
   London Residence 271
   London Townhouse 137
   Mayfair Pied-à-Terre 147
   Parisian Pied-à-Terre 122
Allard, Jules 184–5, 277
Alnwick Castle, Northumberland 170, 232
Amanda Nisbet Design 64
Apfel, Iris 78
Apfel Residence, New York City 78
Art Deco 9
Art Nouveau 9
Arts and Crafts 9
Asolo Residence, Veneto 16–17
Astaire, Fred 7

B

Baldwin, Billy 11
   Park Avenue Apartment 41
Baratta, Anthony
   Baratta Apartment 48
   Captiva Island Residence 202
   Pink House 109
   Southern California Château 262
Baratta Apartment, Miami 48
Barneys 7, 8
Barrett, Susan 142, 225
Barwon River House, Melbourne 98, 174, 259, 275
Baxter, Anne 7
Beistegui, Carlos de 149
Bel Air Mansion, Los Angeles 150, 222–3
Bellagio Residence, Los Angeles 120
Bendet, Stacey 263
Bennison, Geoffrey 256
Bergamin, Sig 116–17
Bergé, Pierre 257
Bikoff, Sasha 63
Blakeney, Justina 13
   Southern California Home 46
Blenheim Palace, Woodstock 187
Bonetti, Mattia 92

Bore, Richard 100
Brandolini D'Adda, Countess Cristiana 105
Brighton Pavilion, East Sussex 168
Britt, Thomas 13
   New York Apartment 218
   Pied-à-Terre, San Francisco 141
Brooklyn Apartment (James Aguiar) 77
Brooklyn Townhouse (Nick Olsen) 27
Bruce, Liza 213
Brutalism 9
Buatta, Mario
   Aileen Mehle Residence 42–3
   Manhattan Apartment 118–19, 238–9
   Mehle Residence 252–3
   Patricia Altschul Residence 80
Buckingham Palace, London 18
Burch, Tory 229

C

Cabrol, Roger de 67
Caldwell Apartment, New York City 209
Caligula 8
Captiva Island Residence 202
Carraro Residence, Rome 186
Casa Casuarina, Miami 31, 146
Casa Navàs, Reus 96, 198–9
Casa No Name, San Miguel de Allende 254
Casa Vicens, Barcelona 162
Castillo de Chapultepec, Mexico City 136
Castle Schönbrunn, Vienna 30
Cavalli, Eva 22, 132–3
Cavendish, William George Spencer 272
Chanel 234
Château de Chambord 68, 230
Chateau de Chantilly 34
Château de Groussay, Montfort-l'Amaury 149
Château du Champ de Bataille, Eure 21, 72, 140, 189
Château Verrières-le-Buisson 244
Chatsworth House, Derbyshire 272
Chicago Mansion 274
Cindy Adams' Apartment, New York City 268
Collector's House, Seville 226, 249, 264–5
Collett, Anthony 26
Columbo, Joe 165
Couturier, Robert 23
Cowles, Fleur 7
Cox, Sam 180
Cypress Grove, San Francisco 250–1

D

Daigre, Jean-François 33
Dark Ages 8
Davies, Marion 7
Dawnridge, Beverly Hills 6, 7, 40, 76
Dazey, Dani 101, 112, 207

De Gournay Showroom, Paris 106
de la Renta, Oscar 255
de la Renta Apartment, New York City 255
Deering, James 74
Denning & Fourcade
   New York Apartment 32
   Upper East Side Apartment 110
Desmond, Norma 7
di Biasi, Frank 206
Díaz Mori, José de la Cruz Porfirio 136
DiMattio, Francesca 35, 245
Disco Volante 221
Domènech i Montaner, Lluís 96, 198–9
Donnan, Simon 175
Doodle, Mr. 180
Doodle House, Tenterden 180
Doonan, Simon 129, 201, 240
Draper, Dorothy 13
   Greenbrier Hotel 51, 58, 144–5, 203
Drottningholm Palace, Stockholm 97
Dunaway, Faye 130
Duquette, Beegle 7
Duquette, Tony 10
   Dawnridge 6, 7–8, 40, 76
   Duquette Ranch 216
   Manhattan Penthouse 231
   Palazzo Brandolini 183, 190
   Wilshire Corridor Penthouse 151
Duquette Ranch, Malibu 216

E

East Village Loft, New York City 67
Egyptians 8
Eisner, Lisa 7
Elkann, Lapo 90
Esherick, Wharton 193
Eva Cavalli Home, Florence 22, 132–3
Evans, Paul 11

F

Family Lodge, Adirondack Park 236–7
Farmhouse, Turin 73
Ferdinand II 121
Fifth Avenue Apartment, New York City 38–9
Forsblom, Brock 177
Francis II of Bourbon 200
Frederick the Great, King 242
Freud, Sigmund 219
Freud House, London 219
Fulk, Ken 250–1
Futurism 9

G

Gambrel, Steven 276
Garbo, Greta 7
Garcia, Jacques 21, 72, 140, 189
Garrett, Daniel 170, 232
Gaudí, Antoni 162
Gaultier, Jean Paul 10
Gavnø Castle, Zealand 212
Gehry, Frank 10
Georgian Shooting Lodge, Hampshire 179
Georgis, William 214
Getty, Ann 13
   Getty Residence 44–5, 104, 182, 267, 273
   Pacific Heights Residence 20, 208
Getty Residence, San Francisco 44–5, 104, 182, 267, 273
Gili, Oberto 73
Goldschmied, Michela 16–17
Goldwyn, Liz 7
Graceland, Memphis 61, 62, 81, 155, 172–3
Grange, Jacques
   La Datcha 257
   Paris Apartment 192
Gray, Dorian 9
Greeks 8
Greenbrier Hotel, White Sulphur Springs 51, 58, 144–5, 203
Griffith, Gwynn 258
Grisanti & Cussen 91
Grisanti Residence, Santiago 91
Guérard family 25
Gutfreund, Susan 38–9
Gwen, Alisha 65

H

Hacienda Buena Fe, San Miguel de Allende 154
Haines, Billy 13
   Sunnylands 261
Hardouin-Mansart, Jules
   Palace of Versailles 28–9
   Trianon Palace 88–9
Harte, Sheldon 148
Haynes-Roberts 163
Hearst, William Randolph 248
Hearst Castle, San Simeon 248
Heissmann, Harry 178
Heliogabalus 8
Herod, Lindsey 56–7
Hicks, Ashley 47
Hicks, David 7
Holzman, Joseph 50
Hong Kong Apartment 92
Horizon Apartment, Sydney 176
House of Hackney 79, 114, 171
Houston Home 56–7
Huet, Christophe 34
Hunt, Richard Morris 184–5, 277
Huston, Anjelica 7

I

Industrial Revolution 8

J

Jaipur, Maharajah of 228
Jaipur City Palace 36–7, 228
Jaipur Jewel Apartment 213
James, Edward 233
James, Henry 9
Jamieson, Jimmy 142, 164, 225
Jonathan Adler and Simon Doonan's Apartment, New York City 129, 175, 201, 240
Jones, Inigo 123
Jorge Pardo Residence, Brooklyn 205
Joseph Holtzman Installation, New York City 50

K

Kagan, Vladimir 49
Kagan Apartment, New York City 49
Kaihoi, David
   Family Lodge 236–7
   Upstate New York Home 269
Kemble, Celerie 56–7
Kime, Robert 82–3
Kips Bay Showhouse, New York City 63, 135, 214
Kravitz Design 221
Kugelberg, Louise 263
Kuwait Residence (Alidad) 69, 160–1
Kuwait Villa (Alidad) 270

L

La Datcha, Benerville-sur-Mer 257
LA Home, Los Angeles 134
La Torre, Porto Ercole 188
Lapidus, Morris 278
Laurent di Benedetto Residence, Paris 93
Le Vaux, Louis 191
Leemkuil, Brett 70–1
Les Prés d'Eugénie, Eugénie-les-Bains 25
Liberace 7, 196
   The Liberace Museum 127
The Liberace Museum, Las Vegas 127
Liberman, Alexander 7
London House (Anthony Collett) 26
London Northwestern Railway 100
London Pied-à-Terre (Viktor Udzenija) 181
London Residence (Alidad) 271
London Townhouse (Alidad) 137
Los Angeles Farmhouse 220
Louis XIV 6–7, 28–9
   Château de Chambord 68, 230
Lovag, Antti 108
Lovato, Demi 220
Ludwig II of Bavaria 9
   Neuschwanstein Castle 75, 169
Lyford Cay Club House, Nassau 19
Lynch, Kelly 7

M

McMillen Inc 210–11
Madonna 10
Mahdavi, India 13
   De Gournay Showroom 106
Mahdavi, Maryam 152, 167
Malibu Home, Los Angeles 139
Manhattan Apartment (Haynes-Roberts) 163
Manhattan Apartment (Mario Buatta) 118–19, 238–9
Manhattan Apartment (Stacey Bendet and Louise Kugelberg) 263
Manhattan Penthouse (Hutton Wilkinson and Tony Duquette) 231
Manhattan Residence (Tony Burch) 229
Manhattan Townhouse (Francesco DiMattio) 35, 245
Marble House, Newport 184–5, 277
Marcant Home, Belgium 204
Maria Theresa 30
Marino, Peter 13
   Woody House 126, 128
Martyn Thomson Studio, New York City 102–3
Mattel, Trixie 10
Mayfair Pied-à-Terre, London 147
MC Hammer 10
Mehle Residence, New York City 252–3
Melbourne House 246
Memphis Group 10
Meyer, Gene 206
Miami House 107
Mid-Century Modernism 9
Mies van der Rohe, Ludwig 10
Milan Residence 90
Mishaan, Richard 247
Molyneux, Juan Pablo 227
Mongiardino, Renzo
   Carraro Residence 186
   La Torre 188
Monkton House, Chilgrove 233
Montez, Maria 7
Morgan, Julia 248
Morris, William 9
Mountbatten, Lady Pamela 7

N

Nash, John
   Brighton Pavilion 168
   Buckingham Palace 18
Natale, Greg
   Barwon River House 98, 174, 259, 275
   Horizon Apartment 176
   Melbourne House 246
   Toorak Penthouse 113
Neiman Marcus 8
Nero, Emperor 8
Neuschwanstein Castle, Hohenschwangau 75, 169
New York Apartment (Denning & Fourcade) 32
New York Apartment (Miles Redd) 224
New York Apartment (Richard Mishaan) 247
New York Apartment (Thomas Britt) 218
New York City Residence (Robert Couturier) 23
Nisbet Residence, New York City 64
Nureyev, Rudolf 24, 84
Nussbaumer, Michelle
   Hacienda Buena Fe 154
   Nussbaumer Residence 143
Nussbaumer Residence, Dallas 143

O

Old Royal Naval College, London 156–7
Olsen, Nick 27
Oudejans, Marie-Ann 99

P

Pacassi, Nikolaus 30
Pacific Heights Residence, San Francisco 20, 208
Paine, James 170, 232
Palace of Versailles 6–7, 13, 28–9, 191
Palais Bulles, Théoule sur Mer 108
Palazzo Brandolini, Venice 183, 190
Pampelonne, Rose Anne de 53
Pardo, Jorge
   Jorge Pardo Residence 205
   Reyes Residence 52
Paris Apartment (Alberton Pinto) 153
Paris Apartment (Geoffrey Bennison) 256
Paris Apartment (Jacques Grange) 192
Paris Apartment (Maryam Mahdavi) 152, 167
Paris Apartment (Rose Anne de Pampelonne) 53
Paris Apartment (Rouge Absolu) 111
Paris Apartment (Rudolf Nureyev) 24, 84
Paris House (Valerian Rybar and Jean-François Daigre) 33
Parish-Hadley 20, 208
Parisian Pied-à-Terre (Alidad) 122
Park Avenue Apartment (Billy Baldwin for Diana Vreeland) 41
Park Avenue Apartment (Cindy Adams) 217
Park Avenue Residence (Frank di Biasi & Gene Meyer) 206
Parsons, Louella 7
Parton, Dolly 86
Patricia Altschul Residence 80
Pebble Beach Residence 227
Pedro Espirito Santo Residence, Lisbon 125
Pembroke, Earl of 123
Pena Palace, Sintra 121
Peretti, Elsa 188
Pied-à-Terre, San Francisco 141
Pink House, New York City 109
Pinto, Alberto 153
Planting Fields Foundation, Oyster Bay 59
Polo, Roberto 195
Port Lympne Mansion, Kent 124
Postmodernism 9–10
Presley, Elvis 61, 62, 81, 155, 172–3
Private Residence, Gibsonia 65
Pyne, Anne 210–11

Q

Queens Apartment, New York 70–1

R

Redd, Miles 13
   Family Lodge 236–7
   New York Apartment 224
   Upstate New York Home 269
Redd Kaihoi 166, 241
Renaissance 8
Reyes Residence, Playa De Naguabo 52

Roberto Polo Residence, Toledo 195
Roman Penthouse, Rome 115
Romans 8
Ross, Tracee Ellis 7
Rothschild, Baron Ferdinand de 138
Rouge Absolu 111
Royal Palace of Caserta, Campania 200
Rybar, Valerian 33

S

St. Louis Guest House 142, 164, 225
Saks 8
Samuel, Henri
   Château Verrières-le-Buisson 244
   Fifth Avenue Apartment 38–9
San Antonio Factory Residence 258
San Francisco House 148
Sánchez de Moya, Amaro 226, 249, 264–5
Santo, Pedro Espérito 125
São Paulo Estate 116–17
Sassoon, Sir Philip 124
Sawai Jai Singh II, Maharaja 36–7
Scheerer, Tom 19
Schloss Sanssouci, Potsdam 242
Shellhammer, Bradford 66
Shelter Island House 243
Sitwell, Edith 7
Smallwood Architects 179
Smeets, Job 60, 266
SoHo Holiday House, New York City 178
Sommers, Ruthie 274
South Wraxall Manor, Wiltshire 82–3
Southern California Château, Los Angeles 262
Southern California Home, California 46
Stallone, Sylvester 107
Stamp, Terence 7
Street-Porter, Tim 7
Studio Job Headquarters, Antwerp 60, 266
Sultan Osman III 94
Summer House, Orange County 66
Sunnylands, Palm Springs 261
Swanson, Gloria 7

T

Teo Leo Galerie 93
Terry, Emilio 149
Tessin, Nicodemus the Elder 97
Tessin, Nicodemus the Younger 97
Thompson, Martyn 102–3
Thornhill, Sir James 156–7
Thott, Count Otto 212
Toorak Penthouse, Melbourne 113
Topkapi Palace, Istanbul 94
Trematon Castle, Saltash 79, 114, 171
Trianon Palace, Versailles 88–9
Trixie Motel, Palm Springs 10, 101, 112, 207
Turbeville, Deborah 254

U

Udzenija, Viktor 181
Upper East Side Apartment (Denning & Fourcade) 110
Upper East Side Apartment (Steven Gambrel) 276

Upper East Side Townhouse (Anne Pyne, McMillen Inc) 210–11
Upstate New York Home (Miles Redd and David Kaihoi) 269
Upstate New York Home (Redd Kaihoi) 166, 241

V

Valentino 115
Vanbrugh, Sir John 187
Vanilla Ice 10
Vega, Nicholas Alvis 213
Venturi, Robert 10, 11
Versace, Donatella 85
Versace, Gianni 31, 146
Versace Apartment, Milan 85
Victoria, Queen 100
Victorian 9
Villa Palladio, Jaipur 99
Villa Trianon, Versailles 260
Villa Vizcaya, Miami 74
Vilmorin, Louise de 244
Visiona I, Milan 165
Vistorta, Pordenone 105
Voltaire 8
Von Teese, Dita 95, 215
Von Teese Residence, Los Angeles 95, 215
Voorjans, Gert 194
Voorjans Home and Studio, Antwerp 194
Vreeland, Diana 11, 41, 158

W

Waddesdon Manor, Aylesbury 138
Wales, Prince of 168
Warhol, Andy 10, 54
Wearstler, Kelly
   Bel Air Mansion 150, 222–3
   Bellagio Residence 120
   LA Home 134
Wenzeslaus von Knobelsdorff, Georg 242
West Village Apartment, New York City 177
Wharton, Edith 9
Wharton Esherick Studio, Township 193
Whistler, Rex 124
Wilde, Oscar 9
Wilkinson, Hutton 7
   Caldwell Apartment 209
   Dawnridge 40, 76
   Duquette Ranch 216
   Malibu Home 139
   Manhattan Penthouse 231
   Palazzo Brandolini 183, 190
   Wilshire Corridor Penthouse 151
Williams Residence, Beverly Hills 221
Wilshire Corridor Penthouse, Los Angeles 151
Wilton House, Wiltshire 123
Wolfe, Elsie de 6, 13
   Planting Fields Foundation 59
   Villa Trianon 260
Woody House, Long Island 126, 128
Wynant, Marc-Antoine 204

Y

Young Huh Interior Design 135

PUBLISHER'S ACKNOWLEDGEMENTS

The publisher would like to acknowledge the invaluable contributions of the following people, without whom this book would not have been possible: Tim Balaam, Sarah Bell, Vanessa Bird, Clive Burroughs, Beth Dufour, Kate Sclater, Rosie Pickles, and Phoebe Stephenson.

SIMON DOONAN

Writer, media personality, and iconic window dresser Simon Doonan worked for Diana Vreeland at the Costume Institute before joining Barneys New York in 1986, where for nearly three decades he was the creative director behind the store's legendary displays. He is a judge for the NBC show *Making It*, and has been published in the *New York Observer*, *The Daily Beast*, *Harper's Bazaar*, *Glamour*, and *Slate*, among others.

Phaidon Press Limited
2 Cooperage Yard
London E15 2QR

Phaidon Press Inc.
65 Bleecker Street
New York, NY 10012

phaidon.com

First published 2023
© 2023 Phaidon Press Limited

ISBN 978 1 83866 692 7

A CIP catalogue record for this book is available from the British Library and the Library of Congress.

All rights reserved. No part of this publication may be reproduced, stored in a retrieval system or transmitted, in any form or by any means, electronic, mechanical, photocopying, recording or otherwise, without the written permission of Phaidon Press Limited.

Commissioning Editors: Virginia McLeod & William Norwich
Project Editor: Virginia McLeod
Production Controller: Andie Trainer
Design: Hyperkit

Printed in China

PICTURE CREDITS

Every reasonable attempt has been made to identify owners of copyright. Errors and omissions notified to the Publisher in writing will be corrected in subsequent editions.

Melanie Acevedo: 143; David S. Allee: 67; Brittany Ambridge/OTTO: 56-57, 64, 135; © Francis Amiand: 111; The Annenberg Foundation Trust at Sunnylands: 261; Architectural Digest/© Condé Nast: 32, 33, 107; Gavin Ashworth/The Preservation Society of Newport County: 184-185, 277; Photo: Rasid Necati Aslim/Anadolu Agency/Getty Images: 219; © Giorgio Baroni Designed by PINTO: 153; © Bayerische Schlösserverwaltung, www.kreativ-instinkt.de; Norman Barrett/Alamy Stock Photo: 75; Photo: Jonathan Becker for Vanity Fair: 105; Fernando Bengoechea: 183, 190; © James Brittain: 156-157; Simon Brown, House & Garden © Condé Nast: 179; Marco Cantile/Getty Images: 200; © Chateaux de Versailles et de Trianon, Versailles, France/RMN-Grand Palais /Dist. Photo SCALA, Florence: 191; Pascal Chevallier/The Licensing Project: 257; Mark Cocksedge/House of Hackney: 79, 114, 171; Studio Joe Colombo/Ignazia Favata: 165; Country Life/Future Publishing Ltd.: 124; © Roger Davis/OTTO: 53, 78, 120, 139, 141, 150, 222-223, 227, 262; Dani Dazey, @danidazey: 101, 112, 207; DEA/A. DAGLI ORTI/Getty Images: 212; Photo: DeAgostini/Getty Images: 212; Noe DeWitt/OTTO: 166, 236-237; Roop Dey/Alamy Stock Photo: 228; Jacques Dirand/The Interior Archive: 271; Francois Dischinger/Trunk Archive: 134; Photo: Francesco Dolfo/Production: Benedetta Rossi Albini: 22, 132-133; Image provided courtesy of Dorothy Draper & Company, Inc: 51, 58, 144-145, 203; © Frederic Ducout Photography: 93, 152, 167, 195, 204; Andreas von Einsiedel/Alamy Stock Photo: 233; Holger Ellgaard, Reproduced under the terms of the Creative Commons AttributionShare Alike Licence, CC BY-SA 3.0, via Wikimedia Commons. With approval of The Royal Court, Stockholm: 97; ELVIS™ and ELVIS PRESLEY™ are trademarks of ABG EPE IP LLC Rights of Publicity and Persona Rights: Elvis Presley Enterprises, LLC© 2023 ABG EPE IP LLC: 61, 62, 81, 155, 172-173; EPhotocorp | Dreamstime.com: 36-37; Pieter Estersohn/The Art Department: 19, 27; Miguel Flores-Vianna/The Interior Archive x Trunk Archive: 224; Floto+Warner: 70-71; Scott Frances/OTTO: 42-43, 80, 118-119, 238-239, 252-253; Douglas Friedman/Trunk Archive : 154, 250-251, 263; Photo: Gareth Fuller/PA Images/Alamy Stock Photo: 180; © OBERTO GILI: 73; Oberto Gili/Condé Nast/Shutterstock: 256; Roger Jeffrey Isaac Greenberg 8+/Alamy Stock Photo: 136; Roger Guillemot/Connaissance des Arts / akg-images: 244; Francis HAMMOND: 28-29; Paul Harris/Getty Images: 127; Visko Hatfield: 20, 38-39, 208; © Hearst Castle®/CA State Parks: 248; Hemis/Alamy Stock Photo: 108, 149; Robin Hill courtesy of Vizcaya Museum and Gardens: 74; Jeff Hirsch/New York Social Diary: 49, 218; Jim Holden/Alamy Stock Photo: 168; Horst P. Horst, House & Garden © Condé Nast: 110, 115, 255; Horst P. Horst/© Condé Nast/Architectural Digest: 41; Images Cedides per Casa Navàs: 96, 198-199; Stephen Kent Johnson/OTTO: 206, 217, 268; John Kellerman/Alamy Stock Photo: 230; Andrey Khrobostov/Alamy Stock Photo: 68; Nikolas Koenig/OTTO: 52; Ricardo Labougle: 226, 249, 264-265; Francesco Lagnese (Woody House Designed by Pietro Cicognani): 126, 128; Francesco Lagnese/OTTO: 148, 209, 231, 274; David A. Land/OTTO: 65; Manuel Litran/Getty Images: 260; Ana María López: 91; Manolo Yllera/Photofoyer: 129, 175, 201, 240; James McDonald/Interior Archive: 69, 137, 147, 160-161, 170, 232, 270; Joshua McHugh: 243; Konstantin Mironov/Alamy Stock Photo: 169; © Michael Mundy 2021: 50; Noe DeWitt/OTTO: 241, 269; Photo: Alise OBrien: 142, 164, 225; Isabel Parra: 205; Jenna Peffley/OTTO: 46, 220; Eric Piasecki/OTTO: 276; Planting Fields Foundation: 59; Tim Street-Porter: 40, 76, 151, 216; Prussian Palaces and Gardens Foundation Berlin-Brandenburg/Leo Seidel: 242; Paul Raeside/OTTO: 181; Rebecca Reid: 106; Ricardo Labougle © The World of Interiors: 254; RMN-Grand Palais /Dist. Photo SCALA, Florence: 34; Lisa Romerein/OTTO: 44, 104, 273, 276; Photo: Peter Rymwid/Harry Heissmann Inc: 178; Eric Sander: 21, 72, 140, 189; Nicholas Sargent: 63; Alfredo Garcia Saz/Alamy Stock Photo: 88-89; Stefano Scata/The Interior Archive: 16-17; Annie Schiechter/Interior Archive: 77, 109, 177; Annie Schlechter/© Condé Nast: 35, 245; Schmidt/Trunk Archive: 202; Fritz von der Schulenburg/The Interior Archive: 24, 84, 188, 192; Science & Society Picture Library/Contributor, Getty Images: 100; Pete Seaward/Blenheim Palace: 187; Sjankauskas | Dreamstime.com: 94; Anson Smart/Greg Natale: 98, 113, 174, 176, 246, 259, 275; Photo: Peter Smith/Royal Collection Trust/© His Majesty King Charles III 2023: 18; Sotheby's Paris: 45; Studio Job: 60, 266; Christopher Sturman/Trunk Archive: 229; Francis Sultana/Interior Archive: 47; Christopher Simon Sykes/The Interior Archive: 138; Photo: Martyn Thompson. Mural: Dove Hornbuckle: 102-103; Trevor Tondro/OTTO: 66, 95, 215, 221; Tessa Traeger for Robert Kime: 82-83; Photo: Gerhard Trumler/brandstaetter images/Getty Images: 30; Charles Uniatowski/Wharton Eserick Museum: 193; Simon Upton/The Interior Archive: 85, 90, 92, 122, 123, 186, 213, 272; Angel Valentin/Eyevine/The New York Times/Redux: 31; © Tim Van de Velde: 194; Courtesy of Victor Hotels: 146; Frédéric VIELCANET/Alamy Stock Photo: 25; David Vilanova for Airbnb and Casa Vicens Gaudí, 2021: 162; William Waldron/OTTO: 163, 247, 258; Björn Wallander/OTTO: 23, 116-117, 125, 210-211, 214; Floto Warner/OTTO: 48; Mark Luscombe-Whyte/The Interior Archive: 26; Henry Wilson: 99; Manolo Yllera/Photofoyer: 129, 175, 201, 240